Spanish Short Stories

20 Captivating Spanish Short Stories for Beginners While Improving Your Listening, Growing Your Vocabulary and Have Fun

By Sergio Rodriguez

Copyright 2019 - All Rights Reserved — Sergio Rodriguez

ALL RIGHTS RESERVED. No part of this publication may be reproduced or transmitted in any form whatsoever, electronic, or mechanical, including photocopying, recording, or by any informational storage or retrieval system without express written, dated and signed permission from the author.

Table of Contents

INTRODUCTION:	7
CHAPTER 1:	9
"Sueños/Dreams"	9
Questionnaire	10
Translation	11
CHAPTER 2	13
"El último Hombre/The Last Man"	13
Questionnaire	14
Translation	15
CHAPTER 3	16
"Mala Suerte/Bad Luck"	16
Questionnaire	20
Translation	21
CHAPTER 4	25
"El viaje a las Ruinas de los Incas/The trip to the Ruins of the Incas"	25
Questionnaire	28
Translation	29
CHAPTER 5	32
"El Tatuaje Viviente/ The Living Tattoo"	32
Questionnaire	38
Translation	39
CHAPTER 6	45
"Falta de modales a la hora de vestir/Lack of manners when it comes to dressing"	45
Questionnaire	48
Translation	49

CHAPTER 7 — 52

"Los viejos, el árbol y el café/The old men, the tree and the coffee place" — 52
Questionnaire — 53
Translation — 54

CHAPTER 8 — 55

"Crimen/Crime" — 55
Questionnaire — 56
Translation — 57

CHAPTER 9 — 58

"Horrible manera de despertar/Horrible way to wake up" — 58
Questionnaire — 59
Translation — 60

CHAPTER 10 — 61

"Viaje Intergaláctico/Intergalactic travel" — 61
Questionnaire — 63
Translation — 64

CHAPTER 11 — 66

"Alguien me ve/Someone's watching me" — 66
Questionnaire — 67
Translation — 68

CHAPTER 12 — 69

"Clases de Ballet/Ballet classes" — 69
Questionnaire — 70
Translation — 71

CHAPTER 13 — 73
"La casa llena de moscas/The house full of flies" — 73
Questionnaire — 74
Translation — 75

CHAPTER 14 — 76
"Amor a primera vista/Love at first sight" — 76
Questionnaire — 78
Translation — 79

CHAPTER 15 — 81
"El Extraño Libro/The Strange Book" — 81
Questionnaire — 82
Translation — 83

CHAPTER 16 — 84
"La máscara/The Mask" — 84
Questionnaire — 86
Translation — 87

CHAPTER 17 — 90
"El amor de mi vida/The love of my life" — 90
Questionnaire — 92
Translation — 93

CHAPTER 18 — 95
"¿Inocente o culpable?/Innocent or guilty?" — 95
Questionnaire — 97
Translation — 99

CHAPTER 19 — 101
"Vuelve/Come back" — 101
Questionnaire — 101
Translation — 102

CHAPTER 20 — 103
"El Bailarín que Salvó al Mundo/The dancer who saved the World" — 103
Questionnaire — 105
Translation — 105

CONCLUSION — 108

OTHER BOOKS BY SERGIO RODRIGUEZ — 109

Did you enjoy this book? — 110

Introduction:

Have you ever wanted to learn Spanish and have fun at the same time? Most of the time, teaching books are boring. They always have the same kind of format: Two (sometimes more) people talking about where the library is, or where to find Juan.

That's boring, and to be honest, it's not a great way to learn the language (not to mention that they don't always talk about things that you might encounter in your daily life, for example, a judgmental ghost, being the last man on Earth, or maybe find that the love of your life has been stolen).

But in this book, I will give you 20 short stories that will range from science fiction to romance, everything in between and sometimes even more. These stories will give you an entire picture of the Spanish language, and how to appreciate the subtlety of the language.

The Spanish language is rich, full of small differences between the different countries. Things that might be one way in Argentina might be different in Spain or Mexico. But don't worry, with this book, you will have a firm grasp on the language, and you will be able to understand and have a conversation with any Spanish speaker.

After each story, there will be a questionnaire section where you will answer questions about the stories in Spanish. I really suggest to grab a blank page, and write down the answers, or the small assignments that you will be given (don't worry, they won't be long!). Remember to write them in Spanish, so you can practice and use the language. Also, in this section, you will find grammar and fun facts not just from the stories themselves, but from the inspirations behind them, and facts about living in a Spanish country. I hope you like them.

All these stories are written from my heart, and I deeply hope that you will find them funny, mysterious, romantic, or at least entertaining.

That's my goal as a writer, and I hope you enjoy your time reading (and learning!)

Without further a do, here are 20 Captivating Spanish Short Stories for you.

Chapter 1:

"Sueños/Dreams"

Carlos llevó a su hijo a la plaza. Era algo que solían disfrutar los dos cuando hacía buen tiempo. En el medio del parque, había una estatua de bronce de un soldado mirando hacia el horizonte. Debajo de él, había una placa que decía "Sargento Gómez falleció aquí en 1880 luchando por lo que es correcto".

Mientras su hijo jugaba en el arenero, Carlos miraba profundamente a la estatua. Siempre sintió una especie de conexión con ese sargento, aun cuando él llevaba años muerto, y no tenía ninguna conexión familiar. Pero había algo en esa estatua que le llamaba la atención, y no podía decir qué era.

Esa noche, Carlos, luego de cocinarle a su hijo su comida favorita, decidió acostarlo, y luego ver un poco de televisión. Cambió los canales, y en uno de ellos, encontró un documental sobre la guerra de la Independencia. De pronto, el sueño y el cansancio lo vencieron, y se quedó profundamente dormido.

En su sueño, se encontraba en una especie de campo de combate lleno de barro. Había caballos, explosiones y gente corriendo y gritando. De pronto, una explosión lo tiró al piso y lo dejó aturdido. Carlos tenía miedo, todo parecía muy real, y no podía entender qué es lo que estaba pasando.

> Muchacho, arriba, levántese, que tenemos que seguir combatiendo – Una voz amable pero firme sonó detrás de él.

Carlos se dio vuelta y logró ver al Sargento Gómez mirándolo fijamente, con la misma seguridad que tendría en su estatua muchos años después. Como pudo, Carlos se levantó. El Sargento apoyó la mano en su espalda, y le dijo:

Vamos. No me decepcione, que la muerte todavía no nos va a conquistar hoy.

Sorprendido y asustado, Carlos se despertó. Tenía una sensación rara en su cuerpo, como si el sueño hubiera sido real. Trató de olvidarlo, pero no pudo lograrlo. Apagó la televisión, y se dirigió al baño para asearse y prepararse para ir a dormir. En el espejo, vio su reflejo y le sorprendió notar que su cara se encontraba llena de barro. Miró a su alrededor, y notó de que sus zapatos también tenían barro. Pero fue un sueño, no puede haber sido verdad.

Quizás...

QUESTIONNAIRE

- What was Carlos doing in the park?
- Do you have a park close by? If the answer is yes, does it have a statue in the center?
- Have you ever had a dream like Carlos had? What happened?
- In five or six sentences, try to change the ending of the story. Remember, do it in Spanish, and then in English, just to be sure that you understand the vocabulary used.

Let's review some grammar and fun facts!

"Plaza" and "park" are the same word, and in Spanish, they are translated to plaza and parque respectively.

In most countries and main cities, you will find statues and big parks around them. It's very common to see families enjoying their day, reading, or playing football.

Translation

Carlos took his son to the park. It was something that they both used to enjoy when the weather was good. In the center of the park, there was a bronze statue of a soldier watching the horizon. Underneath, there was a plaque that said "Sergent Gomez passed away here in 1880 fighting for what was right."

While his son played in the sandbox, Carlos looked deeply to the statue. He always felt some sort of connection with that sergeant, even though he has been dead for years, and he had no family connection with him. But there was something in that statue that drew attention, and he couldn't say what it was.

That night, Carlos, after cooking his son his favorite food, decided to put him down, and then watch some television. Changed the channels, and, in one of them, he found a documentary about the Independence War. Suddenly, sleep and fatigue defeated him, and he fell profoundly asleep.

In his dream, he found himself in some sort of a combat field full of mud. There were horses, explosions and people running and shouting. Suddenly, an explosion took him to the floor and left him stunned. Carlos was afraid, everything seemed so real, and he couldn't understand what was happening.

> "Lad, up, get up, we have to keep fighting." A kind but firm voice sounded behind him.

Carlos turned around and managed to see Sargent Gomez watching him fiercely, with the same certainty that his statue will have many years later. As he could, Carlos got up. The Sargent put his hand over his back and said,

> "Let's go. Don't let me down, Death will not conquer us today."

Surprised and scared, Carlos woke up. He had a weird feeling in his body like the dream was way too real. He tried to forget, but he couldn't make it. Turned off the television, and went to the bathroom to clean himself up and prepare to go to bed. In the mirror, he saw his reflection and was surprised to note that his face was full of mud. Looked around, and realized that his shoes were also full of mud. But it was a dream, it couldn't be true.

Maybe...

Chapter 2

"El último Hombre/The Last Man"

Miguel se despertó esa mañana repentinamente. Estaba llegando tarde a clases, ya la tercera vez esa semana. No podía ser, si había puesto la alarma correctamente. Se vistió rápidamente, tomó su mochila, y salió corriendo de su casa.

Al llegar a la esquina, notó algo raro: No había nadie en la calle. No solamente gente, sino también autos o animales. Ni siquiera se escuchaban los sonidos de la construcción que estaba a una cuadra de su hogar. Había un absoluto silencio. Extrañado, y un poco asustado, Miguel comenzó a caminar hacia el colegio. No había nadie, y según su reloj, ya debería haber estudiantes en clases. Donde fuera que caminara, no había nadie. ¿Será algún tipo de broma? ¿Algo pasó mientras dormía? ¿Qué es lo que había pasado?

Miguel era fanático de la ciencia ficción, y lo primero que pensó era que toda la gente había sido raptada por extraterrestres. Pero claro, no tenía sentido, porque los extraterrestres no existen. Continuó caminando por todos lados, ya bastante desesperado de que fuera el último hombre sobre la Tierra. Entró a cines, autos abandonados, donde fuera que pudiera encontrar gente, pero no había nadie. Era como si nadie hubiera existido jamás.

A la distancia, un ser extraño lo miraba con sus diez ojos. Extendió sus tentáculos, y estableció conexión con la madre nodriza a través del pensamiento.

> Nos olvidamos de un humano. XCY24 hará contacto y lo eliminará.

Miguel llegó a ver una luz violeta detrás de él, y luego nada más. Al menos no sintió dolor.

Questionnaire

- Have you ever been late to class? What happened?
- Do you live far away from your work?
- If you woke up and found yourself the last human on Earth, what would you do? (I personally would use that time to read all kinds of books!)
- What do you think happened to all the pets and animals?

Let's review some grammar and fun facts!

One example, that we will expand in the next chapter, of words that have two meanings is "*theater*." In Spanish, it can be translated as *teatro* (where you go to see plays from Shakespeare and the like) or as *cine* (where you go to watch movies).

When you are in doubt about what it means, try to search for clues in the context. Most of the time, you can infer the word by looking at the context. But if by any chance you can't do it, and it's a conversation that you are having with someone, ask him what he meant.

TRANSLATION

Miguel suddenly woke up that morning. He was late for classes, the third time that week. That couldn't happen if he had set up the alarm correctly. He dressed up quickly, took his backup and left his house running.

When he reached the corner, he noticed something really strange: There was nobody in the street. Not just people, but also cars or animals. Not even the sounds of the construction a block from his house could be heard. There was an absolute silence. Amazed, and a bit scared, Miguel started walking to the school. There was nobody there, and according to his watch, there should be some students in the class. Wherever he walked, there was nobody. Is this some kind of joke? Something happened while he was sleeping? What has happened?

Miguel was a science fiction fan, and the first thing he thought was that all the people were kidnapped by aliens. But, of course, it didn't make sense, because aliens don't exist. He continued walking everywhere, already really desperate that he was the last man on Earth. He went into movie theatres, abandoned cars, wherever that he might find people, but there was nobody there. It was like no one has ever existed.

In the distance, a strange being watched him with its ten eyes. It extended its tentacles and established a connection with the mothership through its thought.

> "We forgot one human. XCY24 shall make contact and eliminate him."

Miguel saw a purple light behind him, and nothing else. At least he didn't feel pain.

Chapter 3

"Mala Suerte/Bad Luck"

Esteban tomaba el subterráneo todos los días a la misma hora. Durante su viaje, siempre se encontraba con las mismas personas: Mario y Lucía. Ellos eran una pareja amable, que llevaban saliendo alrededor de 5 años. Todas las mañanas, ellos compartían el viaje hacia el centro de la ciudad, y luego, cada uno se dividía para ir a sus trabajos. Esteban trabajaba como diseñador de interiores en una empresa multinacional, mientras que Mario trabajaba en sistemas programando servidores y conexiones de telefonía, y Lucía era maestra de primaria en una escuela cercana.

Un día, Esteban estaba un poco deprimido. Había intentado tener una cita la última semana, pero la realidad es que no fue muy interesante. La chica era de la misma edad que Esteban, pero al llegar al restaurante, ella no dejó de usar el celular en ningún momento. Cuando Esteban intentaba hablar o hacerle alguna pregunta personal, ella contestaba que estaba ocupada, y seguía usando el teléfono. Al final, Esteban decidió pagar la cuenta, e irse temprano a casa. Cuando le dijo esto a la muchacha, no parecía que le importaba mucho.

Bueno, Esteban, tú no tienes suerte con las relaciones, ¿eh? – Dijo Mario, al escuchar la historia al día siguiente.

Sí – Contestó – Creo que voy a morir solo y triste.

¡Vamos, no digas eso! – Le recriminó Lucía – Mira, tengo una propuesta que capaz te interesa. Quiero que vengas a nuestra casa a cenar mañana a la noche.

No sé – comentó triste Esteban – Me parece que tengo planes.

¿Qué planes? ¿Jugar videojuegos toda la noche?

Bueno, es un plan humilde...

Vas a venir, y te aviso, no tomo un no como respuesta.

Al día siguiente, Esteban se debatió mucho entre ir o mentir y decir que estaba enfermo. Al final, decidió bañarse, vestirse e ir. Después de todo, no tenía mucho que perder, y además, él estaba seguro que una fiesta no cambiaría absolutamente nada de su situación. Al llegar, tocó el timbre y esperó. Sintió los pasos detrás de la puerta, y cuando se abrió, se quedó completamente sorprendido: En lugar de que lo recibiera Mario o Lucía, había una mujer pelirroja, con un largo vestido que le llegaba hasta las rodillas, y una sonrisa que inmediatamente lo cautivó.

Perdón, creo que... marqué el timbre equivocado – tartamudeó Esteban

¿Viene a la fiesta de Lucía? Sí, es aquí. Vamos, pasa. Tú debes ser Esteban.

Sí, sí, ¿y tú?

Mi nombre es Andrea, soy una compañera de trabajo de Lucía.

La siguió dentro de la casa, aún sorprendido por la belleza de Andrea. Cuando ingresó al comedor, se encontraban sus amigos esperándolo, ambos con una sonrisa enorme. Mario, al ver la cara de sorpresa de Esteban, no pudo evitar largar una carcajada, que luego tuvo que excusar que era porque se había acordado de un chiste que le habían contado en la semana. Todos se sentaron a comer, y mientras Lucía servía la comida, Mario le hacía preguntas a Esteban sobre su trabajo.

¿Y qué tal te fue en el último proyecto que trabajaste? – Y luego, mirando a Andrea, añadió – Esteban es diseñador de interiores, y la semana pasada nos comentó que estaba trabajando en la reformación de las galerías que se encuentran cerca del museo.

Bueno, eh, no es tan importante como parece – Tímidamente respondió Esteban – Estamos tratando de lograr hacer que esas galerías se puedan utilizar nuevamente, y para esto, bueno, estamos reformando las estructuras y la pintura.

¡Eso suena genial! – Dijo Andrea – A mi novio le encantará saber todo sobre eso.

Se hizo un profundo silencio en la mesa. Lucía la miró con dudas.

Pero... me habías dicho que estabas soltera.

Ah, sí, pero es que nos reconciliamos, y decidimos volver a intentar de nuevo una relación. De todas maneras, no creí que fuera necesario aclararlo. ¿Acaso me invitaste a cenar porque querías que lo conociera a tu amigo?

Sí, de hecho, fue mi idea – Dijo Mario, tratando de calmar la situación – No pensamos que estabas saliendo con alguien – Y mirando a Esteban, añadió – Te pido disculpas.

La cena prosiguió bastante normal. Esteban ayudó a lavar los platos, y cuando estaba por salir, Andrea le pidió si no la podía acompañar mientras esperaba un taxi.

Afuera, ambos comenzaron a conversar.

Sabes... No quiero que sientas que no tendría nada contigo – Dijo Andrea

Entiendo. De todas maneras, la verdad es que la cena fue bastante buena, y con eso me quedo contento.

¿Es cierto que haces diseño de interiores? Porque creo que te puedo ofrecer algo que te gustará.

Por favor, que no sea otro encuentro forzado – Sonrió Esteban. A pesar de todo, le gustaba hablar con ella.

No, no – contestó entre risas- Nada parecido a eso. Toma mi tarjeta, y llámame. Ah, y una cosa más... Realmente me haces reír mucho. ¿Te parece que hablemos para juntarnos en una semana o dos?

Llegó un taxi, y se despidieron rápidamente. Esteban se quedó mirando la tarjeta, pensativo. Bueno, al menos tenía una amiga nueva. Después de todo, no fue una mala idea haber salido de casa.

Questionnaire

- Have you ever had bad luck at a date? What happened?
- Do you have any good friends like Mario and Lucía?
- Write down, in a few sentences, if you had a bad date, and if you did, what you did to change it. Remember, in Spanish!

Let's review some grammar and fun facts!

"Date" in English means two things, but the fun thing in Spanish is that the word also has two meanings in Spanish:

"Date" can be translated as *fecha* (a date, for example, July 10th) or as a *cita* ("Juan and Carlos go out on a date").

There are a lot of words that in Spanish have two meanings. I will give you an example:

muñeca – Doll/Wrist

nada – Swim/Nothing

There are a couple of good jokes about it, for example, the one my daughter always tells me and laughs:

- Un pez se encuentra con otro, y le pregunta qué hace su papá.
- Nada.

The rough translation would be (and keep in mind that in Spanish it's hilarious, but in English it loses some of the charm):

"One fish meets another one, and asks what does his father do."

"Nothing/Swim."

See? There are a lot of words in Spanish that have two meanings. That's why Spanish is fantastic for double entendre jokes.

Translation

Esteban takes the subway every day at the hour. During his trip, he always met with the same people: Mario and Lucía. They were a nice couple, who has been going out for the past five years. Every morning, they shared the ride to the center of the city, and then, they each went their own ways to their jobs. Esteban worked as an interior designer for a multinational company, while Mario worked in IT programming servers and network connections, and Lucía was a primary school teacher in a school nearby.

One day, Esteban was a bit depressed. He had tried to have a date the past week, but the reality was that it wasn't very interesting. The girl was the same age as Esteban, but after arriving at the restaurant, she didn't stop using her cell phone at any time. When Esteban tried to talk or ask her any personal question, she answered that she was busy, and continued using her phone. In the end, Esteban decided to pay the bill and go home early that night. When he mentioned this to the girl, it didn't seem like she cared.

> "Well, Esteban, you don't have any luck with relationships, eh?" said Mario after listening to the story the next day.
>
> "Yeah," he replied. "I believe that I will die alone and sad."
>
> "C'mon, don't say that!" Lucía reproached him. "Look, I have a proposition that might interest you. I want you to come over to our house for dinner tomorrow night."
>
> "I don't know, said Esteban sadly. "I believe that I have other plans."
>
> "What plans? Playing video games all night?"
>
> "Well, it's a humble plan…"
>
> "You are going to come, and I warn you, I don't take a no for an answer."

The next day, Esteban really debated himself between going, or lying and saying he was sick. In the end, he decided to take a shower, get dressed and go. After all, he didn't have much to lose, and also, he was sure that a party wouldn't change absolutely anything of his situation. When he arrived, he rang the doorbell and waited. He heard the steps behind the door, and when it opened, he was absolutely surprised: In place of there being Mario or Lucía, there was a redheaded woman, with a long dress that got to her knees, and a smile that immediately captivated him.

>"Sorry, I think that… I rang the wrong doorbell," Esteban stuttered.
>
>"Are you coming to Lucía's party? Yeah, it's here. C'mon, get in. You must be Esteban."
>
>"Yeah…yeah, and you?"
>
>"My name is Andrea, I'm a work colleague of Lucía's."

He followed her into the house, still surprised by Andrea's beauty. When he entered the dining room, he found his friends waiting for him, both with a huge smile. Mario, when he saw Esteban's surprised face, couldn't suppress a fit of laughter, that then he had to excuse himself saying that he had remembered a joke that he heard during the week. Everybody sat down to dinner, and while Lucía served the food, Mario asked questions Esteban about his work.

>"And how did it go in the last project that you worked on?" And then, watching Andrea, added, "Esteban is an interior designer, and the past week told us that he was working on the reforms of the galleries close to the museum."
>
>"Well, eh, it's not as important as it sounds, timidly, Esteban replied. "We are trying to make it so those galleries can be used again, and for this, we are reforming the structures and painting."

"That sounds great!" Andrea said. "My boyfriend would love to hear everything about that."

A deep silence falls over the table. Lucía looked at her dubiously...

"But... You said that you were single."

"Ah, yeah, but it happened that we got back together, and decided to try a relationship again. Anyway, I didn't think that it was necessary to clarify that. By any chance, did you invite me to dinner because you wanted me to meet your friend?"

"Yeah, in fact, it was my idea," Mario said, trying to calm the situation. "We didn't think that you were dating someone." And looking at Esteban, he added, "I apologize."

The dinner proceeded pretty normally. Esteban helped to wash the dinner plates, and when he was about to go, Andrea asked him if he couldn't be with her while she waited for a cab.

Outside, both started to talk:

"You know, I don't want you to feel that I wouldn't have anything to do with you," Andrea said.

"I understand. In any case, the truth is that the dinner was pretty good, and with that I'm happy."

"Is true that you do interior design? Because I think that I can offer you something that you might like."

"Please, let it not be another forced encounter." Esteban smiled. Despite everything, he enjoyed talking to her.

"No, no," she answered while laughing. "Nothing like that. Take my card, and call me. Ah, and one other thing... You really make me laugh. How about that we talk so we can meet in a week or two?"

A cab arrived, and they quickly said goodbye. Esteban stayed looking at the card, thoughtful. Well, at least he had a new friend. After all, it hadn't been a bad idea to leave the house.

Chapter 4

"El viaje a las Ruinas de los Incas/The trip to the Ruins of the Incas"

Todavía recuerdo la primera vez que realmente pensé en ser arqueólogo. Tenía 10 años y mi padre me había prometido que iba a llevarme al cine si aprobaba todas mis materias. Estudié esa semana como nunca había estudiado antes, y, llegado la hora de los exámenes, los aprobé todos con una excelente nota. Siempre fiel a su palabra, papá me llevó al cine del barrio. Ahí fue cuando vi por primera vez Indiana Jones y Los Cazadores del Arca Perdida. Mientras miraba a Harrison Ford saltando, golpeando a los villanos, encontrando las pistas que lo llevarían a encontrar el Arca de la Alianza, algo dentro mío cambió para siempre: Quería ser él. Quería tener esas aventuras, enamorarme de ese tipo de mujeres, vivir al máximo.

Al llegar a casa, atormenté a mi padre con preguntas. ¿Cómo podía ser arqueólogo? ¿Había que estudiar mucho? ¿Dónde había que estudiar? ¿Qué pasos tenía que seguir?. Mi padre adoptó una actitud que voy a valorar el resto de mi vida, y comenzó a conseguir información al respecto. Él no sabía cómo se estudiaba eso, después de todo, era simplemente un obrero que nunca pudo terminar la secundaria. Pero al ver mis ojos brillando ante la posibilidad de ser como Indiana Jones, él hizo todo lo que se encontraba en sus manos (y aún mucho más) para darme todas las chances necesarias de cumplir mis sueños. Trabajó horas extras, organizamos salidas a la biblioteca para poder leer todo lo que fuera remotamente parecido a la arqueología, me compraba revistas de ciencia e investigación, recortaba partes del periódico donde se detallaban expediciones o avances científicos en la exploración de las pirámides. Incluso logró obtener la dirección de correo postal de un famoso arqueólogo de mi país, y me insistió en que le escriba una carta.

En la carta, le pregunté absolutamente de todo, desde cuáles eran sus teorías sobre quién construyó las pirámides, hasta sobre cuál era la mejor manera de usar un látigo. Quería saberlo todo. La respuesta de la carta tardó un poco en llegar. Cuando lo hizo, 3 meses después de que yo la había enviado, fue un poco escueta. Pero la primera línea de la carta fue lo que más me llamó la atención:

> "Disculpa porque no pude contestar antes, pero es que estaba de viaje en Egipto. Aparentemente, hay una tumba que no podemos explicar el origen"

¡Egipto! ¡Estuvo en Egipto! El resto de la carta eran consejos sobre qué carrera estudiar, y dónde era el mejor lugar para hacerlo. Abracé a mi papá, con lágrimas en los ojos, y le agradecí todo el esfuerzo que hizo para conseguirme esto. De más está decir que ese día los dos lloramos abrazados, y decidimos darnos un gusto comiendo un poco de helado.

Varios años después, me gradué de arqueólogo de la universidad más prestigiosa de mi país, y si bien mi padre había fallecido un par de años antes por culpa de una enfermedad, no podía dejar de sentir una tristeza, pero a la vez felicidad porque logré cumplir la meta que me había puesto desde tan chico. Al poco tiempo de haberme graduado, me ofrecieron un puesto importante de investigación en la Universidad de Oxford.

¡No lo podía creer! Tanto esfuerzo finalmente había rendido frutos. Así que empaqué, y me dirigí hacia Oxford, lugar de mi próxima aventura. Me dieron una oficina, un asistente con el que tenía que trabajar, e incluso me ofrecieron la posibilidad de dar clases. ¿Yo, dando clases de arqueología? No lo podía creer, todo esto era mucho para mí, era como un sueño y yo seguía dormido. Así que la realidad de mi trabajo diario fue la primera que me golpeó en la cara. Todo el día encerrado en una oficina, corrigiendo exámenes, leyendo informes y trabajos de mis alumnos. ¿Dónde estaban mis viajes por las junglas de Sudamérica? ¿Dónde estaban mis villanos muy malos, y las reliquias muy viejas? ¿Acaso era todo mentira?

Decidí juntar dinero, y para mis siguientes vacaciones, irme a explorar las ruinas de los Incas. Subí a un avión, y cuando llegué allá, lo primero que hice fue anotarme en una excursión para visitar las ruinas. Llegué ahí, con mi cincel y un diario para tomar nota, esperando encontrarme con algo que nadie había explorado, con alguna reliquia perdida que había sido ignorada. Pero estaba lleno de turistas con cámaras de fotos, dejando rastros de basura por todos lados. ¿Acaso no entendían que eso podía perjudicar cualquier exploración del lugar que uno quisiera llevar a cabo? Traté de escapar de la multitud de turistas, y me adentré en un camino que decía "Prohibido pasar". Pisé un cúmulo de hojas que parecían haber quedado del anterior otoño, y el suelo se abrió y me envolvió en una profunda oscuridad. Caí en lo que parecía ser un pozo.

Tomé mi encendedor, y lo usé para iluminarme. No había ningún rastro de nada. Era un pozo sin ningún tipo de marca, ni pintura, ni tampoco alguna manera de salir de ahí. Grité y grité, pero nadie logró escucharme. El hambre me hacía doler el estómago, y mis costillas parecían fracturadas, a juzgar por el dolor que sentía. Comencé incluso a dejar de sentir mis extremidades. Hasta que una luz me envolvió, y una voz muy familiar me llamó por mi nombre.

Ven. Ya pasó todo. Ya estás bien. Toma, te traje un poco de helado.

Questionnaire

- What is your favorite movie? Why?
- Have you ever seen any of the Indiana Jones movies?
- Have you ever visited Oxford or do you know someone who studied there?
- Write down a different ending, where the main character, instead of falling into a well, finds an old relic.

Let's review some grammar and fun facts!

In Spanish, funnily enough, the name Indiana Jones isn't translated because names aren't translated for the most part. Juan would be Juan in English, although some people prefer it to translate it anyway. For example:

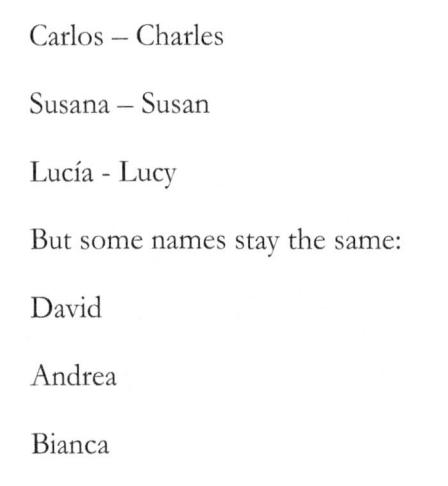

Juan – John

Carlos – Charles

Susana – Susan

Lucía - Lucy

But some names stay the same:

David

Andrea

Bianca

Bruno

TRANSLATION

I still remember the first time that I really thought to be an archaeologist.

I was 10 years old and my father had promised me that he would take me to the movie theater only if I passed all my subjects. I studied that week like I never had before, and, when the exams came, I passed them all with excellent marks.

Always loyal to his word, Dad took me to my neighborhood cinema. It was where I saw for the first time Indiana Jones and the Raiders of the Lost Ark. While I was watching Harrison Ford jumping, punching the bad guys, finding clues that will help him to find the Ark of the Covenant, something inside me changed forever: I wanted to be him. I wanted to have those adventures, fall in love with that kind of woman, live fully.

When I arrived home, I tormented my father with questions. How could I be an archaeologist? Do I have to study a lot? Where should I study? What steps should I follow? My father adopted an attitude that I will appreciate the rest of my life and started to get information on the subject.

He didn't know where to study that. After all, he was just a worker who never finished high school. But when he saw my eyes shining before the possibility of being like Indiana Jones, he did whatever he could (and even more) to give me every necessary chance to fulfill my dreams.

He worked overtime, we organized trips to the library in order to read everything that had a remote connection with archaeology, he bought me science and research magazines, he cut articles from the newspaper where expeditions or scientific advances in the exploration of the pyramids were mentioned.

He even managed to obtain the postal address of a famous

archaeologist of my country, and he insisted I write him a letter.

In the letter, I asked him absolutely everything, from what his theories were about who built the pyramids, to what the best way was to use a whip. I wanted to know everything.

The answer to the letter took a while to arrive. When it did, three months after I had sent it, it was a bit succinct. But the first line of the letter was what jumped to my attention:

"Sorry that I couldn't reply before, but I was on a trip in Egypt.

Apparently, there is a tomb and we can't explain its origin."

Egypt! He was in Egypt! The rest of the letter was advice over what career to study, and where it was the best place to do it. I hugged my Dad, with tears in my eyes, and I thanked everything he did to get this for me. It goes without saying that we both cried while hugging that day, and we decided to get a treat, a bit of ice cream.

Several years later, I graduated as an archaeologist from the most prestigious university in my country, and while my father had passed away a couple of years before because of a sickness, I couldn't stop feeling sad, but at the same time happy because I finally was able to fulfill the goal that I decided when I was a kid. Soon after graduating, I was offered an important research job at the University of Oxford.

I couldn't believe it! So much effort had finally paid off. So I packed up and went to Oxford, the place of my next adventure.

They gave me an office, an assistant with I could work with, and they even offered me the possibility to teach. Me? Teaching archaeology? I couldn't believe it, this was too much for me, it was like a dream and I was still sleeping.

So the reality of my daily job was the first to hit me in my face. All day locked up in an office, grading exams, reading reports and work from my students. Where were the trips through the jungles of South

America? Where were the really bad guys, and the really old relics? Was it all a lie?

I decided to save up some money, and for my next vacations, I went to explore the ruins of the Incas.

I got up on a plane, and when I got there, the first thing that I did was to sign up to an excursion to visit the ruins. I arrived there, with my chisel and a diary to take notes, expecting to find something that no one has ever explored before, with old lost relics that had been ignored.

But it was full of tourists with cameras, leaving trash everywhere. Did they not understand that it could harm any exploration of the place that one might want to perform?

I tried to escape the crowd of tourists, and went into a road that said, "Do not enter." I step over a cluster of leaves that were there from the past autumn, and the floor opened and swallowed me in a deep darkness. I fell in what it looked like a well.

I took my lighter and used it to illuminate my surroundings. There wasn't a sign of anything. It was a well without any kind of mark, paint or any way to get out. I screamed and screamed, but no one could hear me. Hunger made my stomach hurt, and my ribs seemed broken, judging by the pain that I felt. I started to even stop feeling my arms and legs.

Until a light enveloped me, and a very familiar voice called me by my name.

"Come. It's all over. You are all right now. Here, I brought you some ice cream."

Chapter 5

"El Tatuaje Viviente / The Living Tattoo"

Finalmente llevé a cabo la tontera más grande de mi vida. Amigos y familiares me dijeron que no lo haga, incluso mi propia consciencia me insistió que no lo haga. Pero me decidí: Me hice un tatuaje.

Elegirlo no fue fácil. Al principio pensé en hacer algo alegórico a mis gatitos, quizás una patita o algo que me recuerde lo mucho que los quiero. Pero luego, cuando comencé a ver diseños, noté que mucha gente se hacía eso, y la verdad es que no quería seguir la corriente de lo que hacen las otras personas. Siempre me definí como una chica bastante singular y especial, así que lo que menos quería era hacer era seguir la corriente.

Mi búsqueda me llevó a encontrar símbolos tribales, similares a los que tenía mi entrenador personal en el gimnasio. Esos me gustaron mucho más, pero otra vez, mis búsquedas me mostraron que todo el mundo usaba algo parecido. Ya cerca de la frustración y a punto de olvidarme de mi capricho, encontré finalmente lo que quería: Dos estrellas rodeando un animalito dentro. ¡Me encantó! Me parecía muy tierno, y si lograba cambiar y hacer que el tatuador ponga a mis gatitos, iba a quedar muchísimo mejor.

Luego de elegir el diseño, llegó el momento de encontrar el mejor precio para alguien que tiene un presupuesto chico como yo. Cada uno de los tatuadores que visité me pedían una fortuna para lograrlo, y yo no entendía por qué. Después de todo, son simplemente un par de líneas, un poco de dibujo, color, sombras, también adaptar la cara de mis bebés al tatuaje, y por supuesto, hacerlo todo rápido y que quede perfecto. No puede costar tanto.

Por suerte, encontré en un barrio abandonado, cerca de un cementerio, en un día donde llovía muchísimo, y sólo pude darme cuenta porque un trueno iluminó el cartel que indicaba que había un tatuador que cobraba poco dinero por su trabajo. ¡Qué casualidad! Cuando entro, el tatuador me mira fijamente. Tenía una barba larga, y una mirada penetrante. Me miró de arriba abajo, y me preguntó si quería un tatuaje.

¿Cómo supo eso?

Porque soy un tatuador. La gente no entra acá buscando información de los partidos de fútbol.

Ah, claro – Contesté- ¿Puede tatuarme este dibujito, pero con unos gatitos?

Le mostré el dibujo que quería. El hombre primero miró el dibujo, y luego me miró fijamente. Suspiró profundamente, con un cansancio que parecía como si estuviera al borde de su paciencia. Al final de su suspiro, que me pareció que duró años, me invitó a pasar a otra habitación donde tenía las herramientas. Había decidido que lo quería en la parte baja de mi espalda, así que me levanté la remera y dejé que trabajara. Mientras él preparaba sus elementos, yo me sacaba fotos para compartir con mis amigos. Cuando intenté sacarle una foto al tatuador, él sólo levantó la mirada, resopló, y siguió trabajando. Me parece que no le gusté.

Finalmente terminó, y pude verme en el espejo. ¡Qué increíble que estaba mi tatuaje nuevo! ¡Encima hizo que mis gatitos tengan los ojos rojos, justo algo que hace que les resalten sus hermosas narices! Le pagué al señor, y me fui contenta del lugar. Cuando me di cuenta de que me faltó tomarme una foto con el señor, giré y me di cuenta que el local no estaba más. ¡Qué raro! Bueno, no importaba, yo tenía un tatuaje nuevo.

Al llegar a mi casa, noté que mi vecino otra vez estaba escuchando música muy fuerte. Discutí varias veces con él la última semana, y todas esas veces terminaron conmigo llorando muy frustrada. Intenté juntar fuerzas para golpearle la puerta y prepararme para discutir, pero el cansancio era mucho mayor. No pensé que tener un tatuaje iba a cansarme tanto, nadie me había dicho nada al respecto. Le di de comer a mis gatitos, y me acosté. Ni siquiera logré llegar a cambiarme, que el sueño y el cansancio me sobrepasaron. Estaba tan cansada, que ni siquiera el ruido de mi vecino fue suficiente para mantenerme despierta. Mis sueños fueron bastante raros, llenos de sombras y figuras oscuras que sentía cerca de mí, y una voz fría que me preguntaba si deseaba ayuda.

Me despertaron mis gatitos arañando asustados mi cara, y cuando abrí mis ojos, sentí una presencia en mi habitación. Al mirar el pie de mi cama, noté una figura alta, llena de huesos y vestido sólo con una túnica negra que flameaba, aunque no hubiera ningún tipo de viento. Cuando habló, note que cada fibra de mi cuerpo temblaba y tenía miedo.

¿Por qué te atreves a despertarme?

¿Yo lo desperté? – Pregunté incrédula

Así es, humana. Dime, ¿cómo lo logró un mero humano como tú?

Asustada, me levanté y me acerqué hacia la puerta de la habitación. Cuando intenté abrir la puerta, la cerradura se trabó y no importara cuánta fuerza hiciera, era imposible abrirla. Estaba encerrada en la habitación con… eso. La figura misteriosa notó mis movimientos y vislumbró mi tatuaje.

Ah, entonces ése fue el método. Esa marca que llevas en la espalda. Debí haberlo sospechado.

¿Mi tatuaje? ¿Qué tiene que ver mi tatuaje?

Soy un espíritu milenario que vivió en el comienzo de la Humanidad. Fui apresado, gracias a la magia negra, en una marca como la que tienes en la espalda. Aunque… la marca original no tenía esos animales.

¡Hey, no digas nada malo de mis gatitos!

Según mi castigo y mi maldición, debo servir y cumplir los deseos de la persona que lleve la marca.

Quedé en silencio. ¿Yo... dar órdenes? Ni siquiera puedo lograr que mis gatitos tomen su medicina.

¿Qué tipo de deseos puedes cumplir?

Los que desees. Puedo crear fuego, por ejemplo, y destruir las aldeas de tus enemigos.

Y al decir esto, levantó una mano huesuda, y en la punta de sus dedos, aparecieron pequeñas llamas de color azul.

Ah... Mira... No sé cómo decírtelo, pero... - Saqué mi encendedor de uno de los cajones de mi mesa de luz y lo encendí - La Humanidad ya tiene control sobre el fuego desde hace muchos años ya.

Huh. Era esperable. También tengo la habilidad de iluminar la cueva más profunda.

De su cara, salieron rayos de luces que lograban apenas iluminar mis sábanas. Simplemente tomé mi celular, encendí la linterna, y se la mostré.

Lo siento, señor Espíritu, pero la verdad es que no me está impresionando. Si no va a hacer nada interesante, le voy a pedir que se retire, por favor.

El espíritu, ya recurriendo a sus últimos trucos que tenía a su disposición, extendió sus brazos, o al menos, lo que parecían ser sus brazos, y en su túnica negra comenzaron a aparecer nebulosas. Cuando habló, su voz parecía más lejana y profunda.

No quería llegar a esta demostración, humana, pero no me dejas ninguna otra opción. Pregúntame lo que desees saber, y puedo ofrecer la respuesta en cuestión de horas.

Comencé a sentirme mal por el señor Espíritu. Claramente estaba intentándolo, pero no podía dejar de notar que sus habilidades ya no eran tan importantes. Tomé de vuelta mi celular, apagué la linterna y abrí la página principal de Google. Giré el celular, y se lo mostré al señor Espíritu. Inmediatamente contrajo sus brazos, y comenzó a investigar el celular.

No entiendo. ¿Quieres decir que tienes acceso a todo el conocimiento humano habido y por haber en... este aparato?

Sí, señor Espíritu.

Entonces... ¿He sido reemplazado?

Lo siento mucho, señor Espíritu.

Largó un suspiro lleno de tristeza. Mis gatitos, como sintiendo qué es lo que le sucedía, se acercaron y comenzaron a ronronearle. Cansado y derrotado, el espíritu se sentó en el borde de la cama, y tomó la cabeza, como si estuviera contemplando la realidad de una Humanidad que ya no lo requería como antes.

¿Sabes? Guerras enteras se han librado por tener mis poderes. Reinos y civilizaciones crecieron y cayeron gracias a mis habilidades. Mi padre me había dicho que esto podía pasarme, pero no pensé que fuera tan pronto. ¡Mírame, todavía soy joven!

No quiero ser ofensiva, pero... ¿cuántos años tiene?

Sólo tengo cien mil años. ¡Todavía soy joven!

Traté de consolarlo, acariciando su espalda y diciendo que todo iba a estar bien. La realidad es que no sabía cómo lograr que se calme. No soy buena calmando a mis amigas, así que menos voy a serlo con un espíritu milenario.

Bueno, señor Espíritu, ya está... Dígame... ¿acaso no tiene alguna otra habilidad especial?

Bueno… Durante estos años, aprendí a cocinar… - Dijo entre lo que sonaban como lágrimas – pero nunca nadie me pidió que les cocine algo. Todos querían destrucción y terror a sus enemigos, ¡y yo soy mucho más que eso!

Al elevar la voz, los cuadros en mi pieza temblaron y se escuchaba que las alarmas de los autos cercanos comenzaban a sonar. Vi, finalmente, una posibilidad de ayudarlo.

¿Sabes cocinar? ¡Eso es genial!

¿En serio?

¡Sí! Yo nunca supe cómo cocinar. Siempre quemé la comida, y nunca pude seguir las más simples instrucciones. Una vez me dijeron que cocinara con sal marina, y pensé que había que ir a la playa para buscarla.

Comenzó a reír. Hasta a mis gatitos les gustó el sonido de esa risa.

Está bien, humana. Puedo cocinarte lo que quieras.

¿En serio? ¡Sí! ¡Muchas gracias, señor Espíritu!

Traté de abrazarlo, pero su forma huesuda me lastimó. Estaba muy feliz. Creo que conseguí un amigo nuevo.

QUESTIONNAIRE

- Do you have a tattoo?
- Be honest: If a millennial spirit appeared in your bedroom, what would you do?
- If you have pets, do they understand you when you are having a bad or a sad day?
- What do they do to cheer you up?
- In as few sentences as possible, try to write what the day to day would be between the protagonist and the spirit. Here's a tip: what kind of food would it cook? Normal food or weird, spiritual food? In Spanish!

Let's review some grammar and fun facts!

In Spanish, we have few words to talk about small kittens: gatito, meaning "little cat" or "kitten." In English, we have several. It is one of the few instances where the opposite is true, since normally, it would happen backwards.

Obviously, there are a lot of ways to talk about kittens in a colloquial way, for example, michi, michifuz, etc.

There are no correct translations for those terms, and since they depend on the place of South America that you are reading about (or talking to someone from), it will always vary. The basic of that sound is the pronunciation of the miau sound, and that's a basis for the michi/michifuz name.

Try to tell your Spanish friends that, and you will find that it's an amazing detail that they probably didn't know!

Translation

Finally, I decided to do the dumbest thing in my life. Friends and family members said that I shouldn't do it, even my own conscience convinced me that I shouldn't. But I was decided: I got a tattoo.

Choosing it wasn't easy. At first, I thought of doing something related to my little kittens, maybe a paw or something that reminds me how much I love them. But then, when I started to see designs, I realized that a lot of people do that kind of stuff and the truth is that I didn't want to go with the flow of what other people do.

I always defined myself as a pretty singular and special girl, so the last thing that I wanted to do is to follow the crowd.

My research took me to find tribal symbols, similar to what my personal trainer at the gym had. Those I liked even more, but again, my research showed me that everybody used something like it.

Close to frustration and on the edge of letting go of my whim, I finally found what I wanted: two stars surrounding a small animal inside. I loved it! It looked so cute to me, and if I managed to change and make the tattooist to insert my kittens, it would look so much better.

After choosing the design, it came the time to find the best price for someone who had a small budget like me. Each tattooist that I visited asked me for a fortune to make it, and I couldn't understand why. After all, it's just a couple of lines, a bit of drawing, color, shadow, also to adapt the faces of my babies to the tattoo, and, of course, doing it quick and perfect. It couldn't cost that much.

Luckily, I found a tattooist. In an abandoned neighborhood, close to a cemetery, one day that rained a lot, and I only realized because thunder lightened up the sign that said that there was a tattooist who charged cheap for his work. What a coincidence! When I went in, the tattooist stared at me. He had a long beard and a penetrating gaze. He looked me up and down, and asked me if I wanted a tattoo.

"How did you know that?"

"Because I'm a tattooist. People don't come in here searching for information on the soccer matches."

"Ah, right, I replied. "Can you tattoo me this little drawing, but with some kittens?"

I showed him the drawing that I wanted. The man first looked at the drawing, and then stared at me. He sighed deeply, with an exhaustion that looked like it was on the edge of his patience.

At the end of his sigh, which seemed to me that lasted years, he invited me to go to the next room where he had his tools. I had decided that I wanted it on the lower part of my back so I lifted up my shirt and let him work. While he prepared his instruments, I took photos to share with my friends. When I tried to take a picture of the tattooist, he only looked up, snorted, and continued to work. I think he didn't like me.

He finally finished, and I could look myself in the mirror. How amazing it looked, my new tattoo!

And he managed to make my kittens have red eyes, exactly what highlights their beautiful noses! I paid the man, and I happily left the place.

When I realized that I forgot to take a picture with him, I turned and realized that the place wasn't there any more. That's weird! Oh well, it didn't matter, I had a new tattoo.

When I arrived home, I realized that my neighbor was again listening to music really loud. I argued with him several times last week, and all those times ended up with me crying really frustrated.

I tried to gather strength to knock on his door and prepared to argue, but the exhaustion was far worse. I didn't think that having a tattoo was going to tire me so much, no one had ever said to me anything like that.

I fed my kittens, and I went to bed. I didn't even manage to change my clothes, sleep and tiredness overwhelmed me. I was so tired, that not even my neighbor's noise was enough to keep me awake. My dreams were really weird, full of shadows and dark shapes that I felt close to me, and a cold voice asked me if I needed help.

My kittens woke me up by scratching my face, and when I opened my eyes, I felt a presence in my room. When I looked at the foot of my bed, there was a tall figure, full of bones and dressed up in a flaring black tunic, even if there weren't any kind of wind. When he spoke, I noticed that every fiber of my body shook and was afraid.

"Why do you dare to wake me up?"

"Did I wake you up?" I asked incredulously.

"That's right, human. Tell me how a human like you managed to do it."

Scared, I got up and got close to the door of my bedroom. When I tried to open the door, the lock got stuck and no matter how much force I used, it was impossible to open it. I was locked up inside my bedroom with… that. The mysterious figure noticed my movements and saw my tattoo.

"Ah, so that was the method. That mark you carry on your back. I should have guessed."

"My tattoo? What my tattoo has to do with you?"

"I am a millennial spirit that lived since the beginning of Humankind. I was jailed, thanks to black magic, in a mark like the one you have on your back. Although… the original mark didn't have those animals."

"Hey, don't say anything about my kittens!"

"According to my punishment and my curse, I must obey and

fulfill the wishes of the person who has the mark."

I was silent. Me… giving orders? I can't even make my kittens take their medicine.

"What kind of wishes can you make?"

"Whatever you want. I can create fire, for example, and destroy the villages of your enemies."

And saying this, he showed a bony hand and, at the tips of his fingers, appeared small blue flames.

"Ah… Look… I don't know how to say it, but…" I took out my lighter from one drawer of my night table and lighted up. "Humankind already has control over fire for a lot of years now."

"Huh. It was to be expected. I also have the ability to illuminate the deepest cave."

From its face, there were rays of light that barely were able to illuminate my sheets. I simply took out my cell phone, turned on the light, and showed it to him.

"I'm sorry, Mr Spirit, but the truth is that you are not impressing me. If you are not going to do something interesting, I'm going to ask you to leave, please."

The spirit, already using his last tricks in his sleeve, extended his arms, or at least, what looked like his arms, and in his black tunic, nebulae started to appear. When he spoke, his voice appeared far away and deep.

"I didn't want to reach this demonstration, human, but you leave me no choice. Ask me anything you wish to know, and I can offer you the answer in a matter of hours."

I started to feel bad for Mr Spirit. It was clearly trying, but I couldn't stop noticing that his skills weren't that important anymore. I took my cell phone again, turned off the flashlight, and opened the Google homepage. I turned the cell phone, and showed it to Mr Spirit. It immediately contracted its arms and started to investigate the cell phone.

> "I don't understand. Are you trying to say that you have access to the entire human knowledge in this… device?"

> "Yes, Mr Spirit."

> "So… I have been replaced?"

> "I'm so sorry, Mr Spirit."

He sighed full of sadness. My kittens, feeling what was happening with him, went closer and started to purr. Tired and defeated, the spirit sat on the edge of the bed and shook his head, like he was contemplating the reality of a Humankind that he didn't know that much anymore.

> "Do you know? Entire wars took place to get my powers. Kingdoms and civilizations grew and fell thanks to my abilities. My father told me this might happen to me, but I didn't think that it would happen so soon. Look at me, I'm still young!"

> "I don't want to be rude, but… how old are you?"

> "I'm only a thousand years old. I'm still young!"

I tried to comfort him, rubbing his back and telling him that everything was going to be alright. The reality is that I didn't know how to calm him down. I'm not good at comforting my friends, and I would be even worse with a millennial spirit.

> "Well, Mr Spirit, it's okay… Tell me… don't you have any other special skill?"

"Well… during all these years, I learned to cook…" He replied between what sounded like tears. "But no one has ever asked me to cook something. They all wanted destruction and terror to their enemies, and I'm much more than that!"

When he raised his voice, the pictures in my bedroom shook and you could listen to the alarms of the closest cars that started to sound. I saw, finally, a way to help him.

"Do you know how to cook? That's great!"

"Really?"

"Yeah! I never knew how to cook. I always burned the food, and I never could follow the simplest instruction. Once they told me that I had to cook with sea salt, and I thought that I had to go to the beach to get it."

The spirit started to laugh. Even my kittens liked the sound of that laugh.

"All right, human. I can cook anything you want."

"Really? Yeah! Thank you so much, Mr Spirit!"

I tried to hug him but his bony shape hurt me. I was so happy. I think I found a new friend.

Chapter 6

"Falta de modales a la hora de vestir/Lack of manners when it comes to dressing"

Para serles honesto, yo no creía en los fantasmas. Cada vez que leía una historia de hechos sobrenaturales, pensaba en que la gente era fácil de engañar, o que confundía hechos con ficción. E incluso, lograba encontrarle una explicación lógica a lo que la gente creía que eran fantasmas o espíritus. Cada vez que leía que había una casa encantada donde los cuadros temblaban, yo pensaba que posiblemente el viento a través de alguna rendija los hacía mover, o que en las cercanías había alguna autopista que generaba ese temblor. Por cada historia de poltergeists, o espíritus demoníacos, yo tenía una respuesta ideal.

Por eso, comencé a escribir varios artículos sobre mis ideas en el periódico local. Esto me dio fama de escéptico, y fui invitado a dar charlas a lo largo de todo el país. La gente solía enfrentarme con sus historias de posesiones, o invitarme a sus hogares donde juraban que en la habitación había fantasmas o que el espíritu de su perrito muerto los visitaba todas las noches. Y ante cada una de estas invitaciones, siempre les daba la respuesta racional e inteligente, y siempre se ofendían conmigo. Me decían que no creía en nada, y que para poder ver los seres del más allá uno tenía que creer en algo.

Por eso, cuando me invitaron al hogar de los Perez, no pensé que iba a ser distinto a lo que ya había experimentado antes. Me habían dejado una nota, y enviado las llaves por correo. En la nota, me daban rienda libre para poder revisar el hogar sin ningún de restricción, y que podía quedarme el tiempo que quisiera. Si decidía irme, sólo tenía que avisar al vecino, que él estaría en contacto con ellos para darles la llave. Empaqué un poco de ropa, y un diario para poder escribir todo lo que encontraba.

Llegué al hogar de los Perez, y la verdad es que de fuera no me parecía muy tétrica. Sí, lucía un poco descuidada, pero nada que un poco de pintura y cuidado no pudieran solucionar. Me elegí una de las habitaciones, y desempaqué. La primera noche no fue muy llamativa, y sólo porque el viento por momentos no me dejó dormir, podría decir que fue una noche muy tranquila. Cuando me desperté al día siguiente, noté que mis camisas y remeras estaban desordenadas, pero eso se podía explicar porque al llegar el día anterior, las había ordenado de cualquier manera Pero, al tratar de ordenarlas, noté que están pegadas a la maleta. Atrás mío, sentí una pequeña risa. Giré y lo vi: Un ser transparente que miraba con una sonrisa burlona.

¿De verdad creías que podías combinar una camisa blanca abierta con una remera de rock pesado? ¿Acaso no te enseñaron nada?

Quedé en silencio. Los Perez no me habían dicho nada sobre qué tipo de fantasma era, simplemente que era muy molesto. La figura me miraba, y esperaba una respuesta. A pesar de mis anteriores experiencias, nunca había visto un fantasma en la vida real. De hecho, todavía seguía sin creerlo.

¿Quién eres? – Pregunté con un tono incrédulo.

¿Ahora? Un fantasma ¿Antes? Diseñador de vestuario. Pero eso no contesta mi pregunta. ¿Acaso no te enseñaron nada de cómo vestirte?

Mira, creo que no tenemos la confianza suficiente como para que me juzgues de esa manera.

Yo voy a juzgar a cualquier persona que se atreva a combinar la ropa de la manera tan horrible que lo hiciste tú.

Pero eres un fantasma, no puedes darme consejos de vestuario.

No sólo no combinas los colores y las texturas de un modo

correcto, sino que, además, no escuchas. Yo era diseñador ¡Diseñador! Yo trabajaba haciendo esto. Los grandes actores de Hollywood requerían mis servicios. Scarlett Johanson, George Clooney, Chris Pratt, Ryan Gosling, Emma Stone

El fantasma continuó enumerando actores famosos a los que les diseñó. Los premios que recibió. Las películas en las trabajó. Y yo no podía dejar de pensar que era demasiado insoportable. Siguió con su discurso durante al menos 5 minutos, y yo estaba seguro que estaba mintiendo.

Mira, señor… señor Fantasma, me convocaron aquí porque me pidieron que investigue si usted era un fantasma de verdad o si había alguna otra respuesta.

¿Entonces?

Bueno, puedo llegar a una sola conclusión: Usted es un fantasma.

Wow, increíble. De verdad eres muy inteligente.

Su tono sarcástico no ayuda a la situación…

Está bien, está bien. Me quedo en silencio.

Gracias. Como decía, usted es un fantasma. Pero no un fantasma cualquiera. Usted es un fantasma insoportable.

La mirada de desilusión del fantasma, debo decir, me partió el corazón.

Oiga, oiga, tranquilo señor. Puedo ofrecerle algo, fantasma.

Lo escucho – Contestó triste el fantasma.

Usted deje en paz a los Perez, yo les daré alguna explicación que los deje contentos, y usted viene conmigo.

Pero… ¿por qué me ofrece eso?

Bueno, usted mismo lo dijo, señor fantasma: Porque no sé vestirme.

Como les decía, yo no creía en los fantasmas. Hasta hace un año. Ahora, si me disculpan, tengo que retirarme. Me invitaron a una fiesta de premiación al mejor vestido del año.

QUESTIONNAIRE

- Do you believe in ghosts or paranormal activities?
- Have you ever seen a ghost? What about a haunted house?
- The ghost in the story is still a costume designer in the afterlife. If that happened to you, what would you be? What kind of profession would you have?
- And if you could switch professions, what would you choose?

Let's review some grammar and fun facts!

In South America, there are a lot of stories about ghosts. One of the most famous is the chupacabra, which isn't exactly a ghost, but no one can actually tell you what it is. Some say it is an animal, others say that it is a spirit, and some people say that it is an experiment made by the government.

Try to compare the supernatural stories from your country or city, to the kind of stories in South America. You will find that they have an amazing tradition on ghosts, possessions and poltergeists.

Translation

To be honest, I didn't believe in ghosts. Every time I read a story of supernatural cases, I thought people were easy to deceive, or they confused facts with fiction.

I manage to find a logical explanation for what people believed were ghost or spirits. Every time I read that there was a haunted house where the pictures shook, I thought that maybe the wind through a crack made them move, or that nearby there was some highway that generated that shake. For each story of poltergeist, or demonic spirits, I had a perfect answer.

Because of that, I started to write several articles about my ideas in the local newspaper. This gave me certain fame as a skeptic and was invited to lecture all over the country.

People used to confront me with their stories of possessions or invite me to their homes where they swore the room had ghosts or that the spirit of their dead dog visited them every night. And to each of those invitations, I always gave them the rational and smart answer, and they always got angry with me. They said that I didn't believe in anything, and to be able to see the afterlife beings you have to believe in something.

That's why, when I was invited to the Perez home, I didn't think it was going to be any different to what I had already experienced.

I had received a note and got the keys by mail. In the note, they gave me free rein to check out the home without any kind of restriction, and I could stay as long as I wished. If I decided to go, I only had to let the neighbor know, and he would be in contact with them to give them the key back. I packed up some clothes, and a diary to write anything that might happen.

I arrived at the Perez home, and the reality is that from the outside it didn't look very scary. Yes, it was a bit ruined, but nothing that a bit of painting and care couldn't fix. I chose one of the bedrooms and unpacked. The first night wasn't very eventful, and apart from wind that didn't let me sleep, I could say that it was a very quiet night.

When I woke up the next day, I noticed that my shirts and t-shirts were messy, but that could be explained because when I arrived the day before, I sorted them out randomly. But, when I tried to tidy them, I noticed that they were stuck to the suitcase. Behind me, I heard a small laugh. I turned and saw it: A transparent being that looked on with a smile on its face.

> "Did you really think that you could combine a white shirt with a heavy metal t-shirt? Haven't they thought you anything?"

I fell into silence. The Perezes hadn't said anything about what kind of ghost it was, just that it was really annoying. The shape looked at me and hoped for an answer. Despite all my previous experiences, I had never seen a ghost in real life. In fact, I still couldn't believe it.

> "Who are you?" I asked with a skeptical tone.

> "Now? A ghost. Before? Costume designer. But that doesn't answer my question. Haven't they thought you anything about how to dress?"

> "Look, I think we don't know each other well enough for you to judge me that way."

> "I'm going to judge anybody who dares to combine clothes the horrible way you do."

> "But you are a ghost, you can't give me clothing advice."

> "You don't only just combine colors and textures in a bad way, but you also don't listen. I was a designer. Designer! I worked doing this. Hollywood's biggest actors required my services. Scarlett Johansson, George Clooney, Chris Pratt, Ryan Gosling, Emma Stone…"

The ghost continued naming famous actors which he had designed for. The awards he received. The movies he worked on. And I couldn't stop thinking that it was too intolerable. It went on with its speech for at least five more minutes, and I was sure that he was lying.

> "Look, mister... mister Ghost, I was invited here because they asked me to investigate if you were a real ghost or if there were any other answers."
>
> "So?"
>
> "Well, I can reach one conclusion: You are a ghost."
>
> "Wow, incredible. You really are smart."
>
> "Your sarcastic tone isn't helping the situation..."
>
> "All right, all right. I will stay quiet."
>
> "Thank you. Like I was saying, you are a ghost. But not just any ghost. You are an insufferable ghost."

The look of disappointment, I have to say, broke my heart.

> "Hey, hey, easy sir. I can offer you something, ghost."
>
> "I'm listening," sadly replied the ghost.
>
> "You leave the Perezes alone, I give them some explanation that makes them happy, and you are coming with me."
>
> "But... why are you offering me this?"
>
> "Well, you said it yourself, mister ghost: Because I don't know how to dress."

Like I was saying, I didn't believe in ghosts. Until a year ago. Now, if you excuse me, I have to go. I was invited to a celebration to the best dressed of the year.

Chapter 7

"Los viejos, el árbol y el café/The old men, the tree and the coffee place"

En el viejo café del barrio, cerca de un antiguo árbol, se solían reunir dos señores de edad mayor. En ese café, trabajé durante todo un verano, tratando de conseguir algunos pesos y poder tomarme unas vacaciones.

La mesa que siempre elegía esa inusual pareja era la mesa que se encontraba justo al lado de la ventana, a donde daba la sombra del árbol. Uno de los dos era ciego, y el otro tenía problemas para caminar, y utilizaba unos bastones. Siempre pedían café con leche, y un vaso de agua. Sus conversaciones parecían muy interesantes, porque siempre se los veía animados, sonriendo, y gesticulando con los brazos.

Un día, me tocó llevarles su pedido. Por alguna razón, quizás un rumor o porque lo había leído en algún periódico, yo estaba seguro que eran escritores. No lo había confirmado, pero mientras le servía el café y el vaso de agua, se los pregunté.

>Disculpen, ¿ustedes son escritores?

El hombre ciego giró su cabeza hacia mí, y me contestó.

>No, nene, somos jugadores de fútbol, y todos los domingos jugamos en el equipo del barrio. Él patea – señalando a su amigo – y yo atajo.

El silencio incómodo inundó el ambiente, hasta que el hombre ciego sonrió y largó la más sonora carcajada que jamás escuché. Una carcajada viva, llena de juventud y alegría. Me retiré de la mesa un poco más tranquilo sabiendo que no los había ofendido.

Al poco tiempo, el ayuntamiento decidió cortar el árbol, ya que consideraban que era muy viejo y que podía caerse en cualquier momento. Llegaron con sus máquinas y lo derribaron. Fue un día muy triste en el barrio. Luego de eso, nunca más volvieron a aparecer el señor ciego y su amigo. Siempre me quedará la duda de si eran escritores o no.

QUESTIONNAIRE

- Do you have any special places to take coffee or eat? What is it like?
- What do you think happened to the odd couple in the story? Do you think they are still alive?
- What do you think the odd couple were? Writers?
- Rewrite the ending to make it a happy ending. Here's a hint: What about the main character? Maybe he searched for them.

Let's review some grammar and fun facts!

Did you know that the characters are based on Ernesto Sábato and Jorge Luis Borges? They were incredible writers, and if you have the opportunity, you should try to read some of their works, which might be a bit hard to understand if you started learning the language, but believe me, they are worth it. They used to have coffee in a small coffee place in San Telmo, Buenos Aires, Argentina.

On the grammar side of this story, we find the usual conundrum between football or soccer. In Spanish, football means the usual sport that we all know, and the NFL and its sports is called American Football, in order to distinguish it from the usual (and far more entertaining, if you ask me!) sports that South American love.

Translation

In the old coffee place of the neighborhood, close to an old tree, two old people used to gather. In that coffee shop, I worked for an entire summer, trying to earn some pesos and go on vacations.

The table that the unusual couple always chose was the table right next to the window, where the shadow of the tree was. One of them was blind, and the other had walking problems and used a special cane. They always asked for coffee with milk and a glass of water. Their conversations seemed very interesting, because they always looked lively, smiling and gesticulating with their arms.

One day, I had to take them their order. For some reason, maybe a rumor or because I had read it in some newspaper, I was sure that they were writers. I hadn't confirmed it, but while I was serving them their coffee and the glass of water, I asked them:

"Excuse me, are you writers?"

The blind man turned his head to me and replied.

"No, kiddo, we are football players, and every Sunday we play in the neighborhood team. He kicks" – pointing at his friend – "and I'm a goalkeeper.

The uncomfortable silence flooded the place until the blind man smiled and had the loudest laugh that I've ever heard. A lively laugh, full of youth and joy. I left the table a bit more calm knowing that I hadn't offended them.

Soon after this, the city council decided to cut down the tree, because they considered that it was too old and it might fall at any time. They arrived with their machines and cut it down. It was a really sad day in the neighborhood. After that, the blind man and his friend never showed up again. I will always have doubt if they were writers or not.

Chapter 8

"Crimen/Crime"

Juan tomó su arma, se levantó de su silla, y salió. Subió a su auto de policía, encendió la radio, y comenzó a patrullar el barrio. Era un barrio bastante tranquilo, donde prácticamente nada sucedía, más allá de algún pequeño robo de bicicletas, o algún altercado entre los niños del colegio secundario que se encontraba a unas pocas cuadras de la estación de policía.

Patrulló durante todo el día. Llegó a su casa, besó a su mujer, y a su hija, cenaron los tres juntos, se duchó y luego se acostaron a ver un poco de televisión antes de dormir. En las noticias, escuchó sobre el enorme aumento del crimen en todo el país. Eso le pareció raro a Juan, quien jamás vio un crimen mayor que alguna discusión familiar.

Al día siguiente, hizo su rutina de todos los días, pero al patrullar comenzó a mirar todo a su alrededor con aire extrañado. ¿Será verdad lo que dicen las noticias todos los días? ¿Era cierto que había caos, y destrucción en cada una de las ciudades de la Tierra? No, no podía ser.

Al llegar al borde del pueblo, subió a una pequeña colina, y se tomó unos minutos para contemplar la ciudad. Quizás estaban equivocados. El crimen estaba allá lejos, fuera de la ciudad, y aquí dentro estaban seguros. Sí, lo más probable era que nunca iba a suceder ahí. No mientras esté Juan. Además, más allá de los problemas menores que a veces pueden suceder, ¿qué tipo de crimen podía pasar en el Paraíso?

QUESTIONNAIRE

- What do you think it happened to Juan?
- Do you believe in Paradise?
- What kind of Paradise do you believe in?
- Write down your version of Paradise, but here's a catch: You have to make it in five sentences or less.

Let's review some grammar and fun facts!

The paradise in Spanish is mostly associated with open fields and green pastures, and not a city. But if you go to some parts of Perú, they will tell you the other way around.

Like we did before, we found names that we cannot translate. If you ever meet a Spanish person, ask him if he or she wants his/her name translated when in a normal conversation. Some people are okay with it, but some people don't like it.

TRANSLATION

Juan took his gun, got up his chair, and got out. Got inside his police car, turned on the radio, and started to patrol the neighborhood. It was a really quiet neighborhood, where practically nothing happened, beyond some small bike theft, or some altercation between the kids of the high school that were a few blocks from the police station.

He patrolled all day. Came home, kissed his wife, and his daughter, had dinner with them, had a shower and then they lay down to watch some television before sleeping. In the news, he heard about the huge increase in crime all over the country. That looked weird to Juan, who had never seen a worse crime than a family argument.

The next day, he did his everyday routine, but when he was patrolling he started to look everywhere with a bewildered look. Was it true what the news said every day? Was it true that there were chaos and destruction in each city on Earth? No, it couldn't be.

When he reached the edge of the town, he went up to a small hill and took a few minutes to contemplate the city. Maybe they were wrong. The crime was far away, out of the city, and here they were safe. Yeah, most likely that it wasn't going to happen there. Not while Juan was there. Besides, leaving aside the small problems that might happen, what kind of crime might happen in Paradise?

Chapter 9

"Horrible manera de despertar/Horrible way to wake up"

El jueves fue un día normal para Esteban. Se levantó, se vistió, asistió a clases, luego almorzó, llegó a casa, se puso a estudiar, luego descansó un poco jugando con la Playstation, Luego cenó con sus padres, se duchó y se acostó para dormir. Un día normal como todos.

Se despertó el día viernes, pero ya de inmediato notó algo raro. No parecía que estaba en su propia habitación. Los posters y las fotos no eran las de él, ni tampoco parecía el mismo diseño de habitación. De hecho, parecía una casa completamente distinta. Trató de vestirse, pero también notó que sus ropas eran distintas, de un tamaño mucho mayor al que normalmente usaba. Al llegar al baño, pudo mirarse al espejo. Esteban, quien era joven y vital, tenía un aspecto demacrado, viejo, como si hubiera dormido durante los últimos sesenta años. Sus manos parecían gastadas, ya arruinadas con el paso del tiempo. No tenía ya dientes, y su pelo era bastante escaso.

Trató de buscar ayuda, donde fuera posible encontrarla. Recorrió la casa rápidamente, o al menos, lo más rápido que sus frágiles huesos le permitieron. Al llegar al borde de una escalera, tropezó y cayó. El dolor lo hizo despertarse.

Esteban abrió los ojos asustado, y revisó su habitación. Todo estaba en orden. ¿Qué era lo que había pasado? Corriendo, fue hacia el baño. Era él, no un señor viejo y feo. Respiró con tranquilidad. Ya había pasado, había sido todo una pesadilla.

QUESTIONNAIRE

- What happened to Esteban?
- Who do you think is the old man?
- Have you ever had a dream that you swore it could have been real?
- Let's say that you woke up and you think you are not in your body: What would you do? What are the first things you would do to see if you are in your body or to find out what happened?

Let's review some grammar and fun facts!

One of the fun things about Spanish is that people use "old man" not as an insult, but as a sign of respect. But not all people like it, so be careful when approaching the subject in a conversation.

For example, one of my closest friend's father hates the term, because it makes him feel useless. So before going out saying "viejo" to everyone you meet, try to understand the other person you are talking to, and see if he will find it very disrespectful or not.

Translation

Thursday was a normal day for Esteban. He got up, got dressed, went to classes, then had lunch, came home, studied, then he rested for a while playing with the PlayStation. After that, he had dinner with his parents, had a shower and laid down to sleep. A normal day like any.

He woke up on Friday, but immediately he noticed something strange. It didn't look like he was in his own room.

The posters and pictures weren't what he had, nor did it look like the same room design. In fact, it looked like a completely different house.

He tried to get dressed, but he also noticed that his clothes were different, of a size much larger than what he normally used. When he reached the bathroom, he could take a look in the mirror. Esteban, who was young and vital, had a gaunt look, old, like if he had slept during the past sixty years. His hands looked worn out, already ruined by the passage of time. He didn't have any teeth left, and his hair was pretty scarce.

He tried to get help, where it was possible to find it. He searched the house quickly, or at least, as quickly as his old fragile bones allowed him. When he reached the end of the stairs, he tripped and fell. The pain made him woke up.

Esteban opened his eyes scared, and check out his bedroom. Everything was in order. What had happened? Running, he went to the bathroom. It was him, not an old and ugly man. He calmly breathes. It already passed, it was just a nightmare.

Chapter 10

"Viaje Intergaláctico/Intergalactic travel"

Tatiana abrió los ojos, respiró profundamente, y trató de distinguir su habitación. El viaje había sido bastante extraño, un poco doloroso, pero al menos fue casi instantáneo. Se encontraba en un momento en un lugar de la galaxia, y luego, en el otro. No recordaba exactamente porqué estaba acá, pero sabía que tenía un objetivo.

Al explorar a su alrededor notó que tenía solamente dos piernas, y solamente dos manos. Era raro, porque le habían prometido que iba a tener más. Pero pensó que quizás era un error de su memoria. Al levantarse, admiró con qué facilidad su cuerpo se adaptó a la gravedad de ese planeta. Probó sus piernas. Primero dobló una rodilla, luego la otra. Con qué facilidad lo hacían aquí. Pensar que estaba acostubrada a no tener rodillas o huesos en absoluto en su galaxia. Bajó hacia el piso inferior del hogar, y decidió ingerir algunos alimentos. Cuando abrió la heladera, vio una pequeña caja de cartón de color blanco con unas letras que decían "LECHE". Eso le recordó algo. Quizás era su propósito. Quizás tenía que ver con su objetivo en la Tierra.

Tomó la caja, y vertió su líquido en el interior de un recipiente de vidrio. Cuando la probó, sus papilas gustativas se activaron con miles de sensaciones distintas. Con que esto era el sabor. Podía comprender por qué los humanos se volvían desesperados por conseguir más y más variaciones de sabores, llegando a mezclar cualquier cosa que se pudiera comer.

Salió del hogar, aun completamente sobrepasada por la mera idea de que existieran tantos sabores en algo tan simple como un líquido blanco, cuando una figura familiar la detuvo.

KVUY89, tienes que volver – dijo esa figura con forma de sombra – Nos equivocamos.

¿A qué te refieres? – Contestó Tatiana asustada

Sí, teníamos que enviarte para que investigues el planeta desde la forma de una vaca, y… bueno, nos equivocamos. Culpo al retraso de la transmisión intergaláctica.

Pero… pero…

Lo siento mucho. De verdad lo siento – Levantó lo que parecían ser sus dedos, e hizo un chasquido.

Tatiana despertó. Se encontraba en un establo con otros animales como ella. Entró un humano con un balde de metal y comenzó a ordeñar a uno de esos animales. No recordaba nada de su breve vida anterior.

QUESTIONNAIRE

- Do you believe in extraterrestrial beings?
- If you do, what are they like, according to you?
- Let's say one of those beings appeared in front of you today, what would happen? How would you react?
- Assuming we get intergalactic travel, where would you want to live, and why? What kind of planet would you choose?
- Write down the kind of planets you would love to visit.

Let's review some grammar and fun facts!

Here is a handy list with the names of the planets in the Solar System and their Spanish translations, just in case you ever want to visit other worlds

Sun – Sol

Mercury – Mercurio

Venus – Venus

Earth – Tierra

Mars – Marte

Jupiter – Júpiter

Saturn – Saturno

Urano – Urano

Neptune – Neptuno

Pluto – Plutón

Yes, I know Pluto isn't a planet anymore, but old habits die hard.

Translation

Tatiana opened her eyes, took a deep breath, and tried to identify her bedroom. The trip had been really strange, a bit painful, but at least it was almost instantaneous. She was on one side of the galaxy and the next one, in the other. She didn't exactly remember why she was here, but she knew she had an objective.

When she explored her surroundings, she noticed that she only had two legs, and just two hands. It was weird because she had been promised that she would have more. But she thought that maybe it was a mistake of her memory.

When she got up, she admired the ease that her body adapted to the gravity of this planet. She tried her legs. First, she bent one knee, then the other one. How easily they do it here. To think that she was used to not having knees or bones in her galaxy. She went down to the lower floor of the home and decided to ingest some food. When she opened the fridge, she saw a small white carton box with some letters that said "MILK." That reminded her of something. Maybe it was her purpose. Maybe it had to do with her objective on Earth.

She left the house, still completely overwhelmed by the mere idea that there existed so many tastes in something as simple as a white liquid when a familiar figure stopped her.

> "KVUY89, you have to go back," said that figure in the shape of a shadow. "We had a mistake."

> "What do you mean?" Tatiana replied, scared.

> "Yeah, we meant to send you to research the planet from the shape of a cow, and… well… we had a mistake. I blame the delay of the intergalactic transmission."

> "But… but…"

"I'm so sorry. I really am." He raised what appeared to be his fingers, and snapped them.

Tatiana woke up. She found herself in a stable with other animals like her. A human with a metal bucket started to milk one of those animals. She didn't remember anything about her previous life.

Chapter 11

"Alguien me ve/Someone's watching me"

Papá siempre nos contaba que se sentía perseguido. Desde que Mamá falleció hace cinco años, Papá no salía de casa. Sin sus anteojos, ya rotos hace años, y con su firme negación a operarse de los ojos, vivía encerrado, viendo televisión y escuchando la radio. Estaba seguro que alguien lo miraba por la ventana todos los días a la misma hora. Siempre se acercaba a la ventana del comedor, y, aunque su visión era muy borrosa debido a la edad, siempre podía distinguir una figura que lo miraba con curiosidad. Todos los días, a las cuatro de la tarde, esa misma figura lo veía sin falta.

Papá ya falleció hace una semana, y me tocaba a mí ir a su casa a buscar sus pertenencias. Entré, y de inmediato el aroma a encierro me embargó. Tantos recuerdos y tantas memorias de este hogar, y Papá ya no estaba para compartirlas con nadie. Mi hijo me ayudó a limpiar la casa. Entre tanto trabajo, olvidé qué hora era. Sonó la alarma del gran reloj del comedor indicando que eran las cuatro de la tarde, la hora en la que Papá decía que alguien lo miraba y lo espiaba.

Juan, ¿puedes ir al comedor a apagar la alarma?

Sí, papá.

Ah, y mientras estás ahí, ¿puedes fijarte si ves alguien por la ventana?

Acá no hay una ventana, hay solamente un espejo.

QUESTIONNAIRE

- Do you have any glasses? (If not, you are lucky. I can't read without mine!)
- Let's assume that you find someone looking at you through a window (like the character in the story) every day at the same time. What would you do?
- Do you have big clocks in your house?
- Do you live in a big house?
- Write down, in ten sentences or less, the kind of house the old man lives in. Does it have any pictures? What about books or plants?

Let's review some grammar and fun facts!

The word "glass" is another one of those English words with three different translations: Vaso, as in glass of water, anteojos for spectacles ("I need glasses to read a book"), and vidrio, as in a glass window ("Here's my glass window"). Be mindful of the context, and like everything, practice will make you perfect.

Translation

Dad always told us that he felt persecuted. Since Mom passed away five years ago, Dad didn't get out of the house. Without his glasses, broken years ago, and with his firm denial to get eye surgery, he lived enclosed, watching television and listening to the radio. He was sure that someone watched through the windows every day at the same time.

He always got close to the dining room window, and, even though his vision was very blurry because of his age, he could always make out a shape that looked at him with curiosity. Every day, at four in the afternoon, the same shape looked at him without fail.

Dad passed away a week ago, and I had to go to his house to search for his belongings. I went in, and immediately the aroma of confinement closed up on me.

So many memories and so many recollections of this home, and Dad wasn't around to share them with anyone. My son helped me to clean up the house. Between that much work, I forgot what time it was. The alarm of the big clock in the dining room went off, indicating that it was four in the afternoon, the hour in which Dad said that someone looked and spying on him.

"Juan, can you turn off the alarm?"

"Yes, Dad."

"Ah, and while you are there, can you check out the window to see if you see someone?"

"There's no window in here, only a mirror."

Chapter 12

"Clases de Ballet/Ballet classes"

Siempre fuimos una familia muy conservadora. Nos criamos con una institutriz llamada Susana, una señora de mucha edad, que insistía que en la familia se estudiara ballet. Decía que era bueno para la personalidad, y que formaba carácter y femineidad. Así que le hicimos caso, y todas las mujeres de la familia estudiaron ballet. Mi abuela, mi madre, y mis hermanas, todas bailaron ballet, y todas ganaron premios internacionales.

Mis hijas, por supuesto, no iban a ser la excepción. Cuando nacieron, Susana las tomó en sus brazos ya viejos, y dijo que serían increíbles bailarinas, que tenían todo el potencial de ser estrellas del ballet. Pero Susana, al poco tiempo, falleció. No podíamos estar sin institutriz, porque tanto mi esposa como yo trabajamos todo el día, así que conseguimos a María, una joven que contaba con excelentes referencias de parte de la agencia de institutrices. Ella era una joven firme pero jovial, y nuestras hijas la amaron enseguida.

Al poco tiempo de que Susana falleciera, las niñas quisieron dejar de ir a las clases de ballet. Decían que no tenía sentido, que ya nadie bailaba eso, y que preferían bailar reggaetón. No, les dijimos varias veces, tenían que continuar con la tradición familiar. Tenían que continuar con el legado de Susana, en honor a todo lo que hizo por nuestra familia. Las niñas se enojaron y protestaron, pero siguieron asistiendo a las clases de Ballet.

Un día nos llamó por teléfono la profesora de las clases de Ballet, quien nos informó que las niñas no ponían atención a las clases, y que perdían el tiempo tratando de bailar otras cosas. Había decidido que era suficiente, que iba a tener una charla seria con las niñas, y que iban a acabar con ese sueño ridículo de no continuar con el mandato familiar.

Llegué a casa temprano del trabajo, y escuché en la habitación de ellas una música muy particular, como si fuera algo tribal o quizás música de baile. Me acerqué sin hacer ningún tipo de ruido, despacio para no llamar la atención sobre mi persona. Cuando abrí la puerta, vi a María bailar reggaetón junto a las chicas. Se las veía muy felices, sin la firmeza y exigencia del ballet. Las veía libres, contentas, alegres como pocas veces había visto en mi vida. Quizás estaba equivocado.

Esa noche tuve una conversación con mi esposa. Que estudien lo que quieran. Que no estén atrapadas en su vida por mandatos de gente que era de otra época.

Que sean felices.

QUESTIONNAIRE

- What was the kind of dance the girls hated?
- And what about the kind they loved?
- Have you ever met a governess?

Let's review some grammar and fun facts!

In South America, it's very normal to have chaperones, but not governesses. And reggaetón is a really popular type of music in South America and parts of Europe. A couple of artists are Pitbull or Wisin and Yandel.

One of my suggestions about learning a new language is to listen to some music on the language that you want to learn. Reggaetón is a good way to do it, while you also dance!

TRANSLATION

We were always a conservative family. We grew up with a governess named Susana, a lady of old age, who insisted that in the family we had to study ballet. She said that it was good for identity and that it shaped character and femininity. So we listened to her, and all the women in the family studied ballet. My grandmother, my mother, and my sisters, they all studied ballet, and they all won international awards.

My daughters, of course, wouldn't be the exception. When they were born, Susana took them on her already old arms and said that they were going to be excellent dancers, that they had all the potential to be ballet stars. But Susana, soon after that, passed away. We couldn't be without a governess, because both my wife and I work all day long, so we hired María, a young lady who had excellent references from the governess agency. She was a young firm but cheerful, and our daughters loved her right away.

Soon after Susana passed away, the girls wanted to stop going to the ballet classes. They said that it didn't make sense, that no one danced that anymore, and that they preferred to dance reggaeton. No, we said several times, they had to continue with the family tradition. They had to continue with Susana's legacy, in honor of all she did for our family. The girls got angry and protested, but they continued to assist the ballet classes.

One day the ballet teacher called us over the phone, and told us that the girls didn't care for the classes and that they wasted their time trying to dance some other dance. I decided that it was enough, that I would have a serious talk with the girls, and that they will have to stop with that ridiculous dream of not continuing the family tradition.

I came home early from work, and I heard from their room a very particular music like it was something tribal or maybe dance music. I got closer without making any kind of noise, slowly so I wouldn't attract attention to myself. When I opened the door, I saw María dancing reggaeton with the girls. They looked so happy, without the firmness and demand of the ballet. I saw them free, happy, full of joy like few times I had seen them in my life. Maybe I was wrong.

That night I had a conversation with my wife. Let them study whatever they want. They shouldn't be trapped in their lives because of other people's mandates that are from another time.

Let them be happy.

Chapter 13

"La casa llena de moscas/The house full of flies"

Mi casa está llena de mosquitos. No importa a qué hora del día ni qué época del año se trate, siempre hay mosquitos de todos los tamaños. Los hay grandes, de esos gordos que molestan a la hora de comer, los hay chiquitos, de esos que no te dejan dormir. Incluso también los había puntiagudos, parecidos a aviones de guerra. Son insoportables.

He intentado de todo. Desde remedies caseros, hasta químicos horribles que estaban más cerca de matarme a mí que matar a los mosquitos. Gasté muchísimo dinero en esos medicamentos, e incluso tuve que pedir prestado dinero para poder lograrlo. Mi familia ya no me visita, porque detestan los mosquitos. Ya estoy harta.

Entro a un vivero, siguiendo el consejo de una amiga, tratando de encontrar algún tipo de árbol que los espante, alguna que desprenda algún olor especial que haga que se vayan y me liberen el hogar. Y, entre tantos árboles y flores de distintos colores, veo una que me llama la atención. Es muy verde, con una especie de dientes, y muy grande. Me enamoró a primera vista.

La llevo a casa, y hasta puedo sentir el miedo de los mosquitos al plantar a mi nueva amiga. Pequeña Boquita, la llamé. Y ayudó muchísimo con los invitados no deseados. A la semana, ya podía dormir tranquilamente. A los tres meses, ya podía dejar comida fuera de la heladera por más de cinco minutos que no pasaría nada. Y mi planta crecía y crecía y crecía. Ahora mide un metro y medio.

La veo en el patio, ya es más grande que yo. Muy verde, muy hermosa, muy grande. Veo una pequeña mosca gorda, una de esas que tanto me hizo la vida imposible durante tanto tiempo. La sigo con la mirada, y veo como se posa dentro de la boquita de mi planta. Me acerco mucho, quiero ver como se la come. Pequeña Boquita cierra su boca, todo se pone muy oscuro. Ya no recuerdo nada.

Questionnaire

- What kind of plant do you think it is?
- Do you like mosquitoes?
- Have you ever been in a vivarium?
- Do you have any plants?
- Write short sentences about what kind of plants you have.

Let's review some grammar and fun facts!

For the ever-expanding list of "words with several translations" (that is the official title, but it's a bit long and not quite catchy):

Fly – volar ("Let's fly to Argentina!") or mosquito/mosca ("I hate this fly!")

Context is important, especially since in this case, we are talking about flying things.

Translation

My house is full of flies. It does not matter what time of the day or which season of the year we are talking about, there are always flies of every size. There are big ones, those fat ones that bother even at lunchtime, there are small ones, those that will not let you sleep at night. Even those that have pointy noses, which look like warplanes. They are unbearable.

I tried everything. From home remedies to horrible chemicals that were closer to killing me than killing the mosquitos. I spent a lot of money on those remedies and even had to borrow money in order to pay them. My family does not visit me anymore, because they hate mosquitos. I am fed up.

I went inside a vivarium, following a friend's advice, trying to find some kind of plant that scares them, any kind that gives off some special smell that makes them go away and free up my home. And, between so many trees and flowers of different colors, I saw one that catches my attention. It's very green, with some kind of teeth, and it was very big. I fell in love at first sight.

I took it home, and I could even feel the fear of the mosquitoes when I planted my new friend. Little Mouth, I name it. And it really helped with the unwanted guests. A week later, I could sleep peacefully. Three months later, I could leave food outside the fridge for more than five minutes and nothing would happen. And my plant grew and grew and grew. Now it is almost 5 feet tall.

I see it in the backyard, already bigger than me. Very green, very beautiful, very big. I see a small fat fly, one of those that made my life impossible for a long time. I follow it with my sight, and I see it pose down inside the mouth of my plant. I get closer, I want to see it how it eats it. Little Mouth closes its mouth. Everything gets dark. I can't remember anything.

Chapter 14

"Amor a primera vista/Love at first sight"

El tren está lleno, es hora pico y todos nos dirigimos a nuestros trabajos. Apretados como si estuviéramos en una lata de sardinas. En medio de la gente, la veo. Ella, con su sonrisa reluciente. Ella, con ese pelo rubio hermoso. Ella, escuchando música y moviendo su cabeza. Y me enamoraste.

Llegamos a una de las estaciones principales, y la gente comienza a descender. Aprovecho para moverme desde donde estaba hacia donde estaba ella se encontraba. Quiero hablarle, quiero presentarme, quiero invitarla a salir. Pero justo cuando a punto de acercarme, mucha gente sube. Me dejan lejos de ella. Al menos mírame. Quiero sonreirte a la distancia. Mírame. Mírame. Mírame.

Girás y nuestras miradas se cruzan. Es en ese momento que te sonrío, y, por esas casualidades del destino, me devolvés la sonrisa. El mundo se me abre debajo de mis pies, y mi corazón salta ante la posibilidad de hablarte. Por supuesto, mi mente se vuelve loca con las posibilidades. Nos veo a nosotros yendo al cine, cenando en un restaurante caro, conociendo a nuestros padres, adoptando un perrito, comprando plantas, mudándonos a un hogar, discutiendo sobre quién cocina, felices porque conseguiste un trabajo nuevo, besándome porque te propuse matrimonio y dijiste que sí, casándonos, festejando, creciendo y envejeciendo juntos.

Te miro, y me pregunto si tendrás novio. Quizás tendrás ganas de conocer a alguien nuevo. ¿Y qué estarás estudiando? Yo diría que estás estudiando medicina o que estás tratando de recibirte de abogada. Miro, a la distancia, si tenés una mochila, o algo así, pero no puedo ver nada que me otorgue una pista de lo que te gusta, ni siquiera una pista de lo que es que te gusta. Qué comida te agrada. Qué es lo que amás hacer.

Nada que me regale una idea de cuál es tu nombre.

Llegamos a otra estación, y recibiste una llamada de teléfono. No voy a escuchar lo que hablás, no soy esa clase de persona, pero escucho tu "Hola!" y me hacen cosquillas el estómago. Tenés una voz muy hermosa.

Ya está, me decido, voy a hablarte. Voy a preguntarte si para ir a tal lugar tengo que bajarme en la siguiente estación. Yo ya sé la respuesta, pero quiero hacerte algún chiste, quizás un poco de charla, algo que me deje hablarte un poco. Capaz hablarte del clima, o algo así.

Llegamos a una estación, y decidiste bajarte.

Te busco desde entonces.

No puedo encontrarte.

QUESTIONNAIRE

- Have you ever taken the subway during rush hour?
- Have you ever fallen in love at first sight?
- Write the perfect ending for you: Do they get together? Does she find him attractive?

Let's review some grammar and fun facts!

In English, you can say that you want to propose to your other half, and everybody will know what you mean. In Spanish, you have to say "propongo matrimonio" (propose marriage) because if you don't, you are just proposing and the speaker doesn't know what are you exactly proposing!

When you say "propongo" you might be saying that we could go out to eat, or to watch a movie, etc. You are proposing a plan, one that you might have to agree with the other person in the conversation.

There was a story about a man from Utah, or at least, that's what one of my closest friends once told me, who came to live in Chile, and had that exact same problem. Obviously, he didn't find it very funny but his girlfriend definitely did!

Translation

The train is full. It's rush hour and we are all going to work. Tight like we were inside a tuna can. In the midst of everyone, I see her. She, with her brilliant smile. She, with that beautiful blond hair. She, listening to music and moving her head. And you charmed me.

We get to one of the main stations, and people start descending. I use this to my advantage and start moving from where I was to where she is. I want to talk to her, I want to introduce myself, I want to ask her out. However, right when I was about to get close, a lot of people come in. They push me away from hee. At least look at me. I want to smile at you from a distance. Look at me. Look at me. Look at me.

You turned your head and we exchange looks. It is in that moment that I smile at you, and, by one of those casualties of destiny, you smile back. The world opens under my feet, and my heart jumps at the possibility of talking to you.

Of course, my mind goes crazy with the possibilities. I see us going to the theater, having dinner in an expensive restaurant, meeting our parents, adopting a little doggy, buying plants, moving to a new home, arguing about who cooks, happy because you got a new job, kissing me because I proposed to you and you said yes, getting married, celebrating, growing old together.

I look at you, and I wonder if you are dating someone. Maybe you want to meet someone new. And what are you studying? I would say that you are going to med school or that you are trying to graduate as a lawyer. I look, from the distance, if you have a backpack, or something like that, but I can't see anything that gives me a clue on what you like, nor even an idea on what it is that you love. What kind of food you like. What is it that you love to do. Nothing that gives me an idea on what your name is.

We arrive at another station, and you get a phone call. I'm not going to listen to your conversation, I'm not that kind of person, but I manage to listen to your "Hello!" and my stomach tickles. You have a very beautiful voice.

That's it, I am decided, I'm going to talk to you. I'm going to ask you if you wanted to go to whatever place I have to off in the next station. I already know the answer, but I want to make a joke, maybe a bit of small talk, something that allows me to talk to you for a bit. Maybe talk to you about the weather, or something like that.

We get to a station, and you decide to get off.

I've looked for you since.

I can't find you.

Chapter 15

"El Extraño Libro/The Strange Book"

Encontré un libro en la biblioteca de mi abuelo. Era rojo, con letras doradas en la tapa, y en el lomo decía "Las Aventuras de Roberto" con letras negras y brillantes. Tenía una pequeña nota en la tapa.

No abrir

Bajo ninguna circunstancia, no abrir.

Mi curiosidad me ganó. Lo abrí. En la primera hoja encontré una nota escrita a mano, con la letra de mi abuelo.

Es tu última chance. No sigas. Desaparecerás.

Nunca fui bueno siguiendo las reglas y los pedidos, así que continué leyendo. La historia era bastante simple: Se trataba de un chico llamado Roberto, que vivía en una ciudad muy parecida a la mía. Estudiaba en un colegio, como el mío. También tenía un mejor amigo, justo igual que yo, y jugaba en el equipo de fútbol local, exactamente como yo.

Tenía el pelo rojo como el fuego, y la misma cara que la mía. Quien sea que haya escrito esto, era muy raro. Pero me encantaba seguir leyendo. En un momento, en la historia, Roberto entró en un hogar. Dentro, encontró cientos, miles de libros.

Hubo uno que le llamó la atención: "Las Aventuras de David". Me sorprendí que fuera mi nombre. Qué raro, pensé. Cuando llegué a la parte del texto donde lo abría, todo se me nubló y desaparecí dentro del libro.

Una figura me miraba fijamente, con el libro de Las Aventuras de David en las manos. Tenía una mirada profunda, penetrante.

Era yo.

Questionnaire

- What do you think happened?
- Have you ever read a book whose main character looked or acted just like you?
- What would you do if you find yourself inside a book?

Let's review some grammar and fun facts!

In Spanish, people say "dorsal" to refer to the book spine, because spine or thorn is "espina." Be mindful of the context, like I always say.

TRANSLATION

I found a book in my grandfather's library. It was red, with golden letters in the front, and in the spine, it said, *The Adventures of Roberto* in black and shiny letters. It had a small note on the cover.

Don't open

Under no circumstance, don't open.

My curiosity won the best of me. I opened it. In the first page, I found a handwritten note, with my grandfather's handwriting.

It's your last chance. Don't proceed. You will be gone.

I was never good following orders and requests, so I kept reading. The story was very simple: It was about a kid named Roberto, who lived in a city very much like mine. Studied in a school, like mine. He also had a best friend, just like me, and played in the local football team, exactly like me.

He had red hair, like fire, and the same face, like me. Whoever had written this, it was very weird. But I loved to read it. One moment, during the story, Roberto entered a home. Inside, he found hundreds, thousands of books.

There was one that called his attention: *The Adventures of David*. I was surprised that it said my name. That's weird, I thought. When I got to the part where it opened, all went foggy and disappeared inside the book.

A figure stared deeply at me, with the *Adventures of David* book in his hands. He had a deep, penetrating gaze.

It was me.

Chapter 16

"La máscara/The Mask"

La máscara cayó, se quebró y se deshizo en miles de pedazos. El terror se apoderó de mí. Era la máscara que usaba mamá cuando era joven para jugar con su padre, mi abuelo. Me la regaló cuando yo era muy chico. Era algo muy preciado para mí. Y ahora yacía en el suelo destrozada, y yo hice lo que pude para no ponerme a llorar.

Llevé los trozos a mi habitación, y tomé pegamento especial. Los apoyé en mi escritorio, encendí mi luz, y comencé a trabajar. Pedazo tras pedazo, los pegué de una manera muy cuidadosa. Tomé todos los recaudos para que nada estuviera fuera de lugar. Me tomó horas, toda una noche entera para poder terminar y dejarla como si fuera nueva. Limpié los restos de pegamento, y la dejé secar mientras yo me acostaba a descansar un poco.

En medio de la noche, me desperté asustado. Había sentido unos pequeños ruidos en el suelo de mi habitación, y era algo raro, ya que no tenía mascotas. Sonaba como si unas uñas se arrastraran por el suelo, y se dirigían hacia mi cama.

Encendí rápidamente la luz y pude ver una imagen fugaz de algo que se movía rápidamente hacia debajo de mi escritorio. Tomé mi linterna que se encontraba en mi mesa de luz, me acerqué y traté de investigar qué era lo que hacía ese ruido extraño. Desde debajo del escritorio, iluminado por mi linterna, pude ver que la máscara, cuyos ojos brillaban con un rojo profundo, me miraban fijamente. La boca, apenas pegada, se abrió, y cuando habló, la voz la sentí dentro de mí. Me pidió que la tomara, y que la usara.

No pude evitarlo.

Estiré mi brazo, la tomé y me la apoyé en la cara. Inmediatamente, desaparecí en una nube. Desperté en una especie de ciudad futurista, donde había seres que tenían en la cara máscaras parecidas a la mía. Se comunicaban con su mente, o al menos, así lo sentía. Sus ciudades eran gigantes, enormes, con varias civilizaciones bajo su dominio. Se habían extendido por las estrellas, y tenían el control sobre las emociones. Caminé por la ciudad, usando el cuerpo que me otorgaba la máscara. En ellas, vi desolación, y vi también locura.

Entré a un edificio que parecía un museo. Tenían expuesto, o al menos así parecía, seres de formas que no entendía, cubos y triángulos con aspecto extraño que flotaban en una especie de líquido que hacía que estuvieran suspendidos en el aire. También podía ver que tenían fragmentos de otros planetas, y de algunos soles.

Seguí caminando, y pude ver carteles con letras extrañas, y lo que parecía ser como automóviles volando en el aire, con muchos de estas máscaras caminando por ahí. No parecía como que las máscaras habían construido esto, sino más bien, habían tomado el control del lugar, quizás tomando posesión de los seres que ya vivían acá. Cuando veo que mi cuerpo me llevaba a algunos barrios, pude notar que había seres que no tenían la máscara, y que tenían marcas en la cara como si la hubieran tenido hace tiempo. Era extraño. Mi cuerpo no me dejó ver más sobre esto, y me llevó al sector donde estarían los infantes.

Ahí estaban en filas, en lo que parecía un colegio, estudiando sobre civilizaciones, estrellas largamente perdidas, y todos, todos de ellos, con la mirada de la máscara encima de sus caras. Caras perdidas, y atentas. Era espeluznante. Comencé a tener muchísimo miedo. Pude reconocer en una placa que parecía ser un pizarrón un sistema solar parecido al nuestro, como se lo mostraría desde el espacio.

El cuerpo me llevó hacia otro sector, el lugar donde estaban los avances científicos. Eran edificios altos, de color blanco, donde se podía ver que experimentaban sobre armas y naves de distintos tamaños. Tenían el conocimiento, o al menos eso me parecía, de poder experimentar con agujeros negros, o la materia en sí misma. Entré en una de las habitaciones más grandes, siempre llevado por el cuerpo que me otorgaba la máscara.

Vi como esa civilización estaba investigando sobre viajes en el tiempo, y cómo, uno de esos seres se subía a una máquina, y desaparecía en el espacio. De alguna manera, supe que la máscara le había informado a los otros seres que nosotros no estábamos listos. Que prepararan las armas mentales, que cuando llegaran, no podríamos hacer nada.

También vi como esa nave caía en la Tierra, hace muchísimos años. Vi como mi Abuelo tomaba la máscara, sin saber su origen. Vi los juegos de mi madre con esa máscara. Y vi, no, sentí el dolor absoluto cuando se cayó al suelo hoy y se partió.

Me saqué la máscara, respiré profundo, tomé un martillo, y la destrocé a golpes.

Espero que con esto sea suficiente.

QUESTIONNAIRE

- What would you do if you find an old mask?
- Write ten sentences that expand the world of the mask.

Let's review some grammar and fun facts!

In this story, we don't have many new words, and none of the words that might have several meanings. But one example might be that "mask" might apply to a mask like in the story (or in the Jim Carrey comedy movie).

Translation

The mask fell, broke and tore into thousands of pieces. The terror took over me. It was the mask that my mother used to play with her father, my grandfather. She gave it to me when I was really young. It was something really precious for me. And now it lay on the floor smashed, and I did what I could to not start to cry.

I took the pieces to my room and grabbed special glue. I left them on my desk, turned on my light, and started to work. Piece by piece, I glued it together in a very careful manner. I took all the precautions necessary to avoid anything to be out of place. It takes me hours, and an entire night to finish it and leave it like new. I cleaned up the glue residue and left it to dry while I laid down to get some rest.

In the middle of the night, I woke up scared. I had heard some small noises on the floor of my bedroom, and it was weird since I did not have any pets. It sounded like if some nails dragged on the floor, and approaching my bed.

I quickly turned on the light and I caught a glimpse of something that went quickly under my desk. I grabbed the flashlight that I had in my night table, got closer and tried to investigate what was doing that strange noise.

From under my desk, illuminated by my flashlight, I could see that the mask, whose eyes were shining with a deep red, stared at me deeply. The mouth, barely glued together, opened up, and when it spoke, I felt the voice inside me. It asked me to take it and use it.

I couldn't help myself.

I stretched out my arm, took it and put it on my face. Immediately, I disappeared in a cloud. I woke up in some sort of futuristic city, where there were beings that had masks like mine on their faces.

They communicated with each other using their minds, or, at least, that's how I felt it. Their cities were gigantic, huge, with several civilizations under their rule. They had extended over the stars, and had control over emotions. I walked all over the city, using the body that the mask gave me. In it, I saw desolation, and I also saw madness.

I walked inside a building that looked like a museum. They were showing, or at least that is what it looked like, beings of a shape that I couldn't understand, cubes and triangles with a strange look that were floating in some sort of liquid that forced them to be suspended in the air. I could also see that they had fragments of different planets, and from some suns.

I kept walking, and I could see billboards with strange letters, and what looked like automobiles flying in the air, with several of these masks walking around there. It didn't look like the masks had built this, but, more like they had taken over the place, maybe taking possession of the beings that were already living in here. When I see that my body took me to different neighborhoods, I notice that there were several beings that didn't have masks, and had marks on their faces like they already had it long ago. It was strange. My body didn't let me see more of this, and took me to the place where the kids would were.

There they were in rows, in what looked like a school, studying about civilizations, stars long forgotten, and all, all of them, with the look of the mask all over their faces. Lost faces, and staring. It was creepy. I started to be very afraid. I could recognize in a plaque that looked like a blackboard a solar system like ours, like one might look at it from space.

The body took me to another sector, the place where the scientific advances were. There were tall buildings, colored white, where one could see that they were experimenting with weapons and ships of different sizes. They had the knowledge, or at least that was what it looked like to me, of being able to experiment over black holes, or the matter itself. I walked inside one of the largest rooms, always carried by the body that the masks allowed me to have.

I saw how that civilization was researching on time travel, and how, one of those beings went into a machine and disappeared in space. Somehow, I knew that the mask had informed the other beings that we weren't ready. That they had to prepare the mental weapons, that when they arrive, there was nothing we could do.

I also saw how that ship fell into Earth, a long time ago. I saw how my Grandfather took the mask, without knowing its origin. I saw my mother playing with that mask. And I saw, no, I felt the absolute pain when it fell down and broke in pieces.

I took off the mask, took a deep breath, grabbed a hammer and smashed into pieces.

I hope that this is enough.

Chapter 17

"El amor de mi vida/The love of my life"

La motocicleta me llevó por toda la ciudad. Era mi vieja amiga. El ruido del motor era muy suave, casi como terciopelo. La compré hace 10 años, y desde entonces que me acompaña a todos lados. La llevé en el primer día de mi trabajo, esquivamos tormentas juntos, me ayudó a conquistar chicas (y conocer a mi actual esposa), e incluso, pude rescatarla cuando la robaron. Recuerdo ese día: Salí de la oficina a las 4 de la tarde, como es usual, y cuando miro hacia donde la había dejado en el estacionamiento, ya no estaba.

Llamé a la policía, puse carteles por todos lados, investigué en los sitios de venta de motocicletas usadas, porque quizás alguien la quería vender. A esta altura, ya no quería justicia, quería a mi motocicleta de vuelta conmigo.

Pasaron 3 meses, y yo seguía sin mi moto. A la noche la extrañaba. Cuando tenía que ir a trabajar, mi primer instinto era ir a mi garaje, ponerme el casco y subirme. Durante esos tres meses, todos los días, sin falta, hacía la misma rutina. Mi motocicleta no podía estar sin mí. Necesitaba mis caricias, mis palabras de cariño. Solíamos charlar cuando volvía del trabajo, donde le contaba todo lo que me sucedía. Incluso, cuando tenía días depresivos, mi mejor remedio era subirme y simplemente andar. Mi motocicleta me entendía, y me contestaba con pequeños rugidos del motor para alegrarme, o contestarme una pregunta.

La necesitaba. Por eso no me sorprendí cuando un jueves, exactamente tres meses desde que la habían robado, abrí la puerta del garaje, y sentí un pequeño ruido familiar. Se me llenaron los ojos de lágrimas. Corrí a abrazarla, y puedo jurarles, aunque sé que no me van a creer, que la moto también estaba llorando. Su pequeño motor me hacía ronroneo.

Inmediatamente la revisé, me fijé que no le faltara nada. Alguna que otra marca, mucho barro, y varias marcas de cigarrillo que me enfurecían. ¿Cómo puede ser que no te hayan cuidado, hermano? Llamé a mi trabajo, me pedí mis vacaciones debido a una emergencia familiar, y me encerré en casa a repararla. Mientras, le contaba todo lo que se había perdido en este tiempo, y mi esposa, fiel y comprensiva, me miraba con una sonrisa enorme. No quiso ayudarme, simplemente saludó a mi moto, y nos dejó solos. Sabía que era algo privado, algo que nos conectaba a los dos.

Luego de varias horas, y con la pintura ya seca y lista para ser estrenada, decidí dar una vuelta. Me subí, me puse el casco, y arranqué.

Cuánto te extrañé, mi querida moto.

No voy a dejar que te vuelva a pasar algo nunca más.

QUESTIONNAIRE

- Have you ever ridden on a bicycle?
- What about a motorcycle?
- Try to write, in five sentences, the point of view from the bike.

Let's review some grammar and fun facts!

We keep adding words that have several translations (at this point, we could write a book about it!). Here's an important example that might help you on a daily basis:

In English, we say bike to refer to two different kinds of transports. In Spanish, those are two words separately:

Bicicleta: the one that Lance Armstrong used

Motocicleta/Moto: a bike with two wheels and an engine. For example, a Honda, Suzuki, etc).

And while we are on the subject of motorcycles, the Harley Davidson bikes that you might have seen in movies or TV shows are called choppers, and in Spanish, there is a word that derives from the original English one: choperas.

But, and here's the fun thing, there's also a size of glass that is named choperas. In English, it's a beer mug. In Spanish, they use choperas. It's a big large glass that is often served really cold and kept in the freezer, and only used when you open a new bottle of beer.

You won't find that kind of glass for wine or water, though. Those are specifically for alcoholic beverages.

TRANSLATION

The motorcycle took me all over the city. It was my old friend. The sound of the engine was really soft, almost like velvet. I bought it 10 years ago, and since then it has gone with me everywhere. I took it on the first day of my job, avoided storms together, it helped me to seduce girls (and meet my actual wife), and, I even rescued it when it was stolen.

I remember that day: I left the office at four in the afternoon, like usual, and when I looked where I had left it in the parking lot, it wasn't there anymore.

I called the cops, posted signs everywhere; I looked on every used bike website because maybe someone wanted to sell it. At this point, I didn't want justice, I just wanted my bike with me again.

Three months passed, and I was still without my bike. I missed it at night. When I had to go to work, my first instinct was to go to my garage, put on my helmet and hop on. During all those three months, every day, without missing a day, I did the same routine.

My bike couldn't be without me. It needed my caresses, my words of love. We used to talk while I got back from work, where I told it everything that happened to me. Even, when I had depressing days, my best remedy was to get on and just ride. My bike understood me and answered me with small growls from the engine to cheer me up, or to answer a question.

I needed it. That's why I wasn't surprised when a Thursday, exactly three months after it had been stolen, I opened up my garage door, and I heard a small familiar noise.

My eyes were full of tears. I went to hug it, and I can swear, even though I know that you are not going to believe me, that the bike was also crying.

Its small engine purred at me. Immediately, I examined it, checking out to see that nothing was missing. It had some marks, a lot of mud and several cigarettes marks that got me really angry. How could it be that they hadn't taken care of you, man?

I called work, I asked for leave due to a family emergency, and locked up at home to repair it. Meanwhile, I told it everything that it had missed during all this time, and my wife, loyal and understanding, watched me with a huge smile on her face. She didn't want to help me; she just waved to my bike and left us alone. She knew it was something private, something that connected us both.

After several hours, and with the paint already dry and the bike ready to be ridden again, I decided to go for a spin. I hopped on, put on my helmet, and started it.

How much I missed you, my dear bike.

I won't let anything happen to you anymore.

Chapter 18

"¿Inocente o culpable?/Innocent or guilty?"

Voy a serles enteramente honesto: Existe la posibilidad de que yo sea el causante de la Tercera Guerra Mundial. Antes que se enojen conmigo, déjenme explicarles.

Estaba aburrido en casa, sin nada que hacer, cuando decidí divertirme. Mi conexión a Internet no funcionaba, y mi computadora no era tan rápida y moderna como para poder instalar algún juego moderno, y la verdad es que ya me había aburrido de leer los textos para el colegio. Eran muy aburridos, y además, no iba a ir al colegio durante dos semanas porque estaba en vacaciones de invierno. Entonces, recordé algo que me había comentado mi padre una vez hace mucho tiempo: que cuando él era joven, se divertían jugando en el patio, o haciendo llamadas de broma.

Bueno, afuera llovía mucho, así que eso ya estaba descartado. Pero la idea de las llamadas broma me encantaba. Tomé la guía telefónica, y marqué el primer número que encontré. Me atendió un señor grande.

> Hola
>
> Eh, sí, hola. Mi nombre es... - Tuve que improvisar – David, y quería saber si cuando abre la canilla, sale agua.
>
> A ver, un momento – No podía creerlo, el señor realmente fue a revisar. Esto no tenía sentido – Sí, está saliendo agua. ¿Por qué lo pregunta?

La risa me ganó. No pude continuar. El señor me dijo varias cosas que, por respeto a todos ustedes, no voy a repetir. Estuve toda la tarde haciéndolo, primero marcando números de la guía telefónica, y ya al final, cuando me estaba aburriendo, números al azar. Ahí fue cuando, en una de esas llamadas, me atendió una voz rasposa y robótica

¿Contraseña?

Eh... Cuando abre la canilla, ¿sale agua?

Un silencio del otro lado de la línea.

Contraseña aceptada.

Y la línea murió. Esto sucedió el... diez de enero. Y todos sabemos qué pasó el día siguiente, ¿verdad?

Señor, le pedimos que, a efectos de claridad, explique qué sucedió al día siguiente.

Está bien, su Señoría. Al día siguiente, Rusia (o al menos, en ese entonces se llamaba Rusia) cerró sus fronteras, y lo que luego sería conocido como la Liga de las Naciones Nucleares lanzó sus misiles nucleares, comenzando una lluvia de destrucción sobre todo lo que tocaban.

Está bien. Hemos oído todo lo que necesitábamos oír.

¿Cómo se declara el acusado?

Inocente, su Señoría. Yo no sabía que mi broma iba a terminar generando semejante desastre. Ni menos pensé que la Humanidad se encontraría al borde de la destrucción. De hecho, yo no disparé los misiles, ni tampoco ordené a los ejércitos luchar, así que, técnicamente hablando, yo soy inocente.

Esta Corte encuentra al acusado culpable. Se lo condena a trabajo forzado en las prisiones atómicas de la Luna. Se levanta la sesión.

QUESTIONNAIRE

- Have you ever made a prank call? Answer in Spanish.
- What was the prank call? Did your victim get mad?
- Let's say you find yourself in a situation just like the main character: Would you say that you are guilty, or innocent?
- What do you think happened on the Moon? What are your thoughts on it?
- Write a different ending where he is found not guilty. Try to get into the character and what he would do in that situation.

Let's review some grammar and fun facts!

The basis of the joke is something an old friend once told me that he used to do it when he was a kid, but the ending is a bit reworked. The original prank included an answer that it was something in the vein of, "Well, what would you expect to come out? Wine?"

That was taken from an old comedy show that was really famous on TV during the 60s, and then expanded into the rest of the continent.

What is funny is that while writing this, I actually got a prank call from some kids, but instead of innocently asking me about my water, they asked me if my fridge was working. Needless to say, I did check out if my fridge was working correctly. The laugh that I heard from this side of the line was too much, and I had to laugh with them.

In the grammar side of the story, in Spanish, dates are written like this:

14 de Febrero

10 de Enero

31 de Diciembre

Putting the day first, and then the month. In English, it's backwards. That brings several problems with the date format. In the USA and some parts of Europe, the day is written MM/DD/YYYY (months, days, and years), but in Spanish, it is written DD/MM/YYYY (days, months, and years).

Here's a handy guide of the name of the months and their respective translation:

January - Enero

February - Febrero

March - Marzo

April - Abril

May - Mayo

June - Junio

July - Julio

August - Agosto

September – Septiembre (some places write it as Setiembre, without the p. That's because the pronunciation of the p in Septiembre is hard for some dialects.

October - Octubre

November - Noviembre

December – Diciembre

TRANSLATION

I'm going to be entirely honest with you: There exists the possibility that I might have caused World War III. Before you get angry with me, allow me to explain.

I was bored at home, without anything to do, when I decided to have some fun. My internet connection didn't work, and my computer wasn't as fast and modern so I could install any recent game, and the truth is that I got bored of reading the books for school. They were very boring, and besides, I wasn't going to go to the school for two weeks since I was in my winter holidays.

Then I remembered something that my father once told me a long time ago: That when he was young, he had fun playing in the backyard, or making prank calls.

Well, it was raining a lot outside, so the backyard was out of the question. But I loved the idea of prank calls. I took out the phone guide and dialled the first number that I found. It answered an old man.

"Hello."

"Eh, yeah, hello. My name is…" - I had to improvise – "David, and I wanted to check that when you turn on your faucet, water comes out."

"Let me see. One moment." I couldn't believe it, the guy actually went to check it out.

"This didn't make sense. Yeah, water is coming out. Why do you ask?"

Laughter overcame me. I couldn't continue. The mister told me several things that, out of respect to all of you, I won't repeat. I spent all afternoon doing it, first dialing numbers from the phone book, and at the end, when I was getting bored, random numbers. That's when, during one of those calls, it answered a raspy and robotic voice

"Password?"

"Eh... When you turn on the faucet, does wáter come out?"

Silence from the other side of the line.

"Password accepted."

And the line went dead. That happened on... January the tenth. And we all know what happened next day, right?

Sir, we ask you to, for the purpose of clarification, explain what happened the next day.

All right, your Honor. Next day, Russia (or at least, during that time it was named Rusia) closed up their borders, and what was later to be known as the Nuclear League of Nations launched their nuclear missiles, starting a rain of destruction over everything they touched.

All right. We heard everything that we needed to hear.

How does the defendant plead?

Not guilty, your Honor. I didn't know that my joke was going to start such a mess. And I didn't think that humankind was going to be at the edge of destruction. In fact, I didn't shoot the missiles, nor did I ordered the militaries to fight, so, technically speaking, I am innocent.

This Court finds the defendant guilty. He is sentenced to forced labor in the atomic jails on the Moon. Court dismissed.

Chapter 19

"Vuelve / Come back"

Veo el resto de comida que dejaste en la mesa. Te extraño. No te vayas. Quiero abrazarte nuevamente. Quiero que te quedes, al menos una noche más.

Perdón. Es mi culpa. Te pido disculpas. No debí gritarte. Volvé. Quiero que nos acostemos los dos, y te acaricie la cabeza mientras vemos alguna película. Quiero que te quedes conmigo. Puedo cocinarte la comida que quieras. No me dejes.

Volvé, pequeño gatito.

Questionnaire

- What were you thinking the story was about before reading the twist ending?
- Have you ever gotten a pet? A cat, fish or a dog?
- Take a blank page, and write down a story about that pet. If you never had one, imagine one.
- Try to do it in Spanish.

Let's review some grammar and fun facts!

My stories almost always involve pets because I love them. I grew up with several cats and kittens, and I can't avoid writing about them.

On the grammar side of the (really short) story, scratch can be translated both as "rascar" ("Scratch my head, please") and "rayar"

("This window is scratched").

One of the fun and interesting things is that in South America, they use a lot of English words that aren't translated, and part of the normal and usual conversation. For example, a DJ scratches a vinyl when he is making some music, right? Well, in Spanish, they don't say "rayar el disco," they just say, "Ese DJ scratcheó el disco!" (That DJ scratched the disk!)

Translation

I see the leftovers that you left on the table. I miss you. Don't go. I want to hug you again. I want you to stay, at least one more night.

I'm sorry. It is my fault. I apologize. I shouldn't have screamed at you. I want us to lie down, and I'd scratch your head while we watch a movie. I want you to stay with me. I can cook any food that you want. Don't leave me.

Come back, little kitten.

Chapter 20

"El Bailarín que Salvó al Mundo/The dancer who saved the World"

La invasión fue fácil de detener. De hecho, tan fácil, que muchos dirían que casi fue una mentira. Verán, un día la Humanidad se despertó y se dio cuenta que no estaba sola en el Universo. Sí, es cierto, habíamos encontrado bacterias, e indicios de vida en Marte y Neptuno, pero nada que sea remotamente parecido a vida inteligente.

Un día nos despertamos, y todos los seres humanos notaron que tenían un ser verde, con pequeños cuernitos, flotando cerca de ellos. En todas partes del mundo, los reportes sobre la aparición misteriosa de estos seres llenaron las tapas de los diarios, y el terror tomó varias víctimas a lo largo del planeta.

Fue horrible. Varios meses de desastres, y caos, hasta que al poco tiempo nos dimos cuenta que esos seres, quienes sean que sea, no nos hacían nada. De hecho, ni siquiera tenían ojos ni oídos, o al menos nada parecido a eso. Simplemente flotaban alrededor nuestro. Algunas personas, incluso, comenzaron a adoptarlas como mascotas. Y al poco tiempo, como muchas otras veces en la historia de la Humanidad, nos acostumbramos y seguimos con nuestras vidas. Básicamente, continuamos peleando, siendo egoístas, luchando el uno contra el otro por las cosas más menores.

Llegó el punto en el que esos seres, apodados Marcianitos (aunque no sabíamos si siquiera si venían de Marte o de alguna otra galaxia), fueron tan parte de la vida cotidiana, que incluso comenzaron a tener programas de televisión, videojuegos, películas, investigaciones científicas, libros escritos al respecto. De hecho, también se pudo verificar que alrededor de cada persona, luego de la aparición de los

Marcianitos, comenzaba a aparecer un aura verde, del mismo tono que el ser extraño. Se pudo verificar rápidamente cuando se revisaron estudios antiguos, y luego, estudios hechos nuevamente. Es como si eso seres realmente sí tenían un efecto entre nosotros.

Y un día, apareció una persona que dijo que sabía cómo eliminarlos. Bueno, no fue la primera. Desde la aparición de los Marcianitos, hubo cientos de personas que ofrecían curas mágicas para solucionarlo, desde meditación hasta pastillas, todo por una módica suma, obvio.

Pero esta persona decía que desde que hizo un baile, se fue su Marcianito. Al principio nadie le creía, pero cuando se le hicieron estudios, se pudo notar que realmente había un cambio en su persona. Por supuesto, al principio se lo trató como fraude, pero la realidad es que él no quería fama, ni tampoco solicitaba dinero (a diferencia de las otras personas que ofrecían curas), y de hecho, sólo ofreció su ayuda porque la gente de su pueblo se lo pidió. Así que al que lo deseaba, podía aprender su baile, totalmente gratis, y enseñarle a otros para que pudieran lograrlo.

Su baile era extraño. No tenía forma, y ni siquiera parecía una coreografía bien pensada. Era más bien mover los brazos y las piernas de manera aleatoria, y listo. No había razón, ni estilo, ni gracia. Él decía que lo había descubierto cuando estaba tratando de aprender un nuevo estilo de baile para el que realmente no servía, y en su frustración, movió las piernas y brazos muy enojado. Y así fue como su Marcianito se fue.

Cientos de personas lo intentaron, grabaron videos y lo compartieron en todas las redes sociales. Miles de personas lo copiaron, logrando que todos sus Marcianitos desaparecieran. Se organizaron festivales de baile y de despedida a los Marcianitos, donde la gente se juntaba, comía, y bailaban. Al poco tiempo, esto llevó a un buen acercamiento entre la gente, que a su vez llevó a entendimientos entre ciudades, luego países, y así, sin disparar un solo tiro, comenzaron a desaparecer las guerras, y de a poco, se pudo ir trabajando por un futuro mejor. Era raro de pensar, pero los Marcianitos y su posterior derrota nos habían cambiado de una manera fundamental, mostrándonos que no sólo no estábamos solos, sino que además, era demasiado inútil seguir combatiendo.

Esta forma de pensar nos llevó a las estrellas, y luego, hacia otras dimensiones. Establecimos contacto con miles de especies, y formamos alianzas. La humanidad creció a pasos agigantados, siempre siguiendo el ejemplo de ese bailarín extraño, que en su frustración, nos demostró que podemos ser mejores.

Y esta es la historia de cómo un bailarín salvó al mundo.

Questionnaire

- What were the creatures like?
- What was the dance like? Have you ever tried it?
- In short sentences, try to rework the ending. But here's a catch: Try to do it in Spanish.

Translation

The invasion was easy to stop. In fact, so easy, that many might say that it was almost a lie. You see, one day, humanity woke up and realized that it wasn't alone in the Universe. Yeah, it's true; we had found bacteria and some signs of life on Mars and Neptune, but nothing that was remotely similar to intelligent life.

One day we woke up, and every human being noticed that they had a green being, with small horns, floating near them. In every part of the world, the reports over the mysterious apparition of these beings filled up the newspaper pages, and the terror took many victims across the planet.

It was horrible. Several months of disasters and chaos, until a bit later we realized that those beings, whoever they were, didn't do anything to us. In fact, they didn't even have eyes or ears, or at least nothing resembling that. They just floated around us. Some people, even, started adapting them as pets. And soon after that, like many other times in the history of Mankind, we got used to it and continued with our lives. Basically, we continued to fight, being selfish, arguing against each other for the most trivial things.

It came to the point that those beings, nicknamed Little Martians (although we didn't even know if they came from Mars or from another galaxy), were so integrated in our daily life, that we even started to have television shows, video games, movies, scientific research, books written about them.

In fact, we could also verify that each person, after the apparition of the Little Martians, started to show a green aura, the same tone of the strange being. It could be quickly checked when they checked out old studies, and then, the same studies done recently. It's like these beings had an effect over us.

And one day, someone said he knew how to eliminate them. Well, it wasn't the first one. From the first appearance of the Little Martians, there were hundreds of people that offered magical cures to fix it, from meditation to pills, all for a small fee, of course.

But this person said since he did his dance, his Little Martian went away. At first, nobody believed him, but when research took place, it could be noted that there was really a change in him. Of course, at first it was treated as fraud, but the reality is that he didn't want any fame, nor asked for money (unlike all other people who offered cures), and in fact, just offered his help because the people of his town asked him to.

So to whoever wished for it, they could learn his dance, completely free of charge, and show other people to teach them to do it.

His dance was strange. It didn't have any shape, and it didn't even look like a well-thought choreography. It was more moving the arms and the legs in a random way, and that's it. It didn't have any reason, nor style, nor grace. He said that he found out when he was trying to learn a new dancing style for which he really wasn't good enough, and in his frustration, moved his legs and arms in anger. And that's how his Little Martian went away.

Hundreds of people tried, they recorded videos and shared it on all social media. Thousands of people copied it, making their Little Martian disappear. Dance and Little Martian goodbye festivals were organized where people gathered to eat and dance. Soon after that, this made people got really close, which in turn led to a really close understanding between cities, and then countries, and just like that, without shooting a single bullet, wars started to disappear, and bit by bit, everyone could start working on a better future.

It was weird to think about it, but the Little Martians and their ulterior defeat had changed us in a fundamental way, not just showing us that we were not alone, but that it was also pointless to keep fighting.

This way of thinking took us to the stars, and then, to other dimensions. We established contact with thousands of species, and alliances were forged. Humankind grew up in gigantic steps, always following the example of that strange dancer, who, in his frustration, showed us that we could be better.

And that's the story about how a dancer saved the world.

Conclusion

I hope you enjoyed your time reading this. All these stories are original, and all these stories come from my heart and my soul. I won't say that all these stories are incredible, or that they are life-changing, because that would be a lie, but I hope that, in at least one of these stories, you found yourself reflected, or at least, represented in at least one of the characters.

And, obviously, you learn a lot in the process! That's my main motivation behind everything that I do, and hope it was good enough for you.

The main takeaway that you should learn from this book is that ghosts really exist. Oh, and there are thousands of words that have two or more translations, and like I said a million times before, you have to understand the context before deciding on what word you should use. Be on the lookout for clues in the words, the tone, and everything in between.

This book took a while to be written, and I researched quite a bit on the appropriate subjects to tackle for beginners, and what genres are the best to teach Spanish. In the end, I went with a lot of sci-fi stories, because I found that those are the best stories to start reading in another language. In fact, that's how I started learning!

I want to thank you, from the bottom of my heart, for not just reaching this point, but for taking the time to finish it. Nowadays, we buy a lot of books and we don't read them, but if you took the time to get here, it means that my hard work was at least interesting enough, and if you learned some words that you didn't know, well, in that case, my job is done.

See you soon.

Other Books By Sergio Rodriguez

Book 1 **Spanish for Beginners: Learn the Basics of Spanish in 7 Days**

Book 1 Link

Book 2 Description here.

Book 2 Link

Book 3 Description here.

Book 3 Link

DID YOU ENJOY THIS BOOK?

I want to thank you for purchasing and reading this book. I really hope you got a lot out of it.

Can I ask a quick favor though?

If you enjoyed this book I would really appreciate it if you could leave me a positive review on Amazon.

I love getting feedback from my customers and reviews on Amazon really do make a difference. I read all my reviews and would really appreciate your thoughts.

Thanks so much.

Sergio Rodriguez

ALL RIGHTS RESERVED. No part of this publication may be reproduced or transmitted in any form whatsoever, electronic, or mechanical, including photocopying, recording, or by any informational storage or retrieval system without express written, dated and signed permission from the author.

Printed in Great Britain
by Amazon